750

Heineken
WORLD
OF GOLF 93

Edited by Nick Edmund

STANLEY
PAUL

First published 1993

1 3 5 7 9 10 8 4 2

© Nick Edmund 1993

Nick Edmund has asserted his right under
the Copyright, Designs and Patents Act, 1988
to be identified as the author of this work

First published in the United Kingdom in 1993 by
Stanley Paul and Company Limited
Random House, 20 Vauxhall Bridge Road,
London SW1V 2SA

Random House Australia (Pty) Limited
20 Alfred Street, Milsons Point,
Sydney, NSW 2061, Australia

Random House New Zealand Limited
18 Poland Road, Glenfield,
Auckland 10, New Zealand

Random House South Africa (Pty) Limited
PO Box 337, Bergvlei, South Africa

Random House UK Limited Reg. No. 954009

A CIP catalogue record for this book is available
from the British Library
ISBN 0 09 178100 0

Designed by Rob Kelland at Allsport
Typeset in Gill and Joanna
Colour reproduction by Colorlito, Milan
Printed and bound in Italy by New Interlitho SpA

PHOTOGRAPHIC CREDITS

Dave Cannon/Allsport: Front Cover (all photos), 10, 12 , 13 , 15, 16, 17 (top left and top right), 18 (lower), 20 (top left), 23, 24, 26 (inset), 28, 30, 32, 33 (inset), 34, 35, 36, 40, 41 (inset), 44, 45, 47, 48 (top), 49, 56, 57, 58 (lower left and main), 61 (right), 62, 78, 82 (top right and lower right), 84 (top right), 91 (left), 92 (top right), 95, 97 (lower), 101, 103 (top), 105, 107, 110, 112 (both), 113, 122 (left), 123 (lower), 124, 125, 129, 139, 143, 153 (inset), 157 (left), 162 (main and inset), 164, 167, 172, 173, 175, (lower), 183, 185, 187 (both), 188, 189, 191, 194, 195, 197, 206 (both), 208, 210, 213, 218 (top), 221 (inset), 222; **Allsport:** 54, 61 (left), 128, 137, 196; **Howard Boylan/Allsport:** 219; **Chris Cole/Allsport:** 118 (both), 119; **Tony Duffy/Allsport USA:** 211; **Steve Dunn/Allsport USA:** (182, 186 (inset); **John Gichigi/Allsport:** 86, 92 (top centre); **Otto Greule/Allsport** USA: 131 (top); **Mike Hewitt/Allsport:** 17 (lower right); **Joe Mann/Allsport:** 154, 159; **Bob Martin/Allsport:** 190; **Steve Munday/Allsport:** Back Cover, 8, 20 (lower left), 26 (main), 32 (inset), 60, 63, 67 (inset), 68, 70, 71, 72 (both), 74 (lower), 75, 81 (both), 82 (lower left), 84 (top left and lower), 92 (top left and lower right), 93, 94, 97 (top), 98 (both), 99, 103 (lower), 109, 110, 122 (right), 123 (top), 131 (lower), 141, 152 (main), 156, 157 (right), 160 (both), 184, 192, 200, 201, 202 (both left), 205, 214, 218 (lower); **Gary Newkirk/Allsport USA:** 20 (bottom right), 43, 48 (lower), 126, 130, 134, 135, 149 (lower), 174, 175 (top), 177 (left), 193; **Steve Rose/Allsport:** 120; **Rick Stewart/Allsport USA:** 19, 147 (main), 148, 150; **Anton Want/Allsport:** contents, 155; **Claus Andersen:** 133; **Carl Carolan:** 18 (top), 116, 117, 177 (right), 178, 179; **Nick Edmund:** 186 (main); **Matthew Harris:** 22, 37, 52, 58 (top left), 66 (main), 74 (top), 88, 90, 91 (right), 111, 147 (left), 165, 166, 168, 198, 199, 203, 216, 220 (main), 223 (both); **Rusty Jarrett:** 21 (lower), 73, 170; **Debbie Newcombe:** 149 (top); **Mark Newcombe:** 83, 96, 114, 115, 180, 207

CONTENTS

Foreword by Renton Laidlaw   5
Introduction by Nick Edmund   7

1

1992: A YEAR TO REMEMBER
Highlights and Reflections   14
The Sony Rankings   22

2

THE MAJORS
THE US MASTERS   26
Roll of Honour   28
The 1992 US Masters   29
Commentary by Lauren St John   38
THE US OPEN   40
Roll of Honour   42
The 1992 US Open   43
Commentary by John Hopkins   50
THE OPEN CHAMPIONSHIP   52
Roll of Honour   54
The 1992 Open   56
Commentary by Derek Lawrenson   64

THE USPGA   66
Roll of Honour   68
The 1992 USPGA   69
Commentary by David Davies   76

3

THE WORLD CUP
Roll of Honour   80
The 1992 World Cup of Golf   81

4

GLOBAL GOLF
EUROPE   88
1992 PGA European Tour Review   90
The 1992 Heineken Dutch Open   97
1992 European Tour Results   100
The World Matchplay Championship   110
1992 WPGE Tour Review   114
The 1992 Weetabix British Open   118
The 2nd Solheim Cup   120
USA   126
1992 US PGA Tour Review   128

1992 US Tour Results   134
1992 LPGA Tour Review   146
The 1992 LPGA Majors   150
AUSTRALIA   152
1992 Australasian Tour Review   154
The 1992 Heineken Australian Open   158
1992 Australasian Tour Results   161
JAPAN   162
1992 Japanese Tour Review   164
Japan's 1992 International Tour   166
1992 PGA Japan Tour Results   167
REST OF THE WORLD   168
Asian and African Tour Results   170
1991-92 South African Tour Review   171
The 1992 Johnnie Walker
    World Championship   172
SENIOR GOLF   174
1992 Senior Review   174
The 1992 Senior Majors   176
AMATEUR GOLF   177
1992 Amateur Review   177
The 27th Curtis Cup   179
The 1992 Amateur and US Amateur   180

5

1993: A YEAR TO SAVOUR

Global Golf: January to December   182
1993 Majors Preview
    by Richard Dyson   194
1993 Heineken World of Golf:
    A Preview by David MacLaren   200
1993 Ryder Cup: A Preview
    by Malcolm Hamer   206

6

GREAT GOLF COURSES OF THE WORLD

GREAT GOLF COURSES OF
THE WORLD   214

All text by Nick Edmund unless otherwise credited

FOREWORD

....

By Renton Laidlaw

The season gets longer, the prize money bigger and the performances of the top players more impressive. Season 1992 belonged to two men - Nick Faldo, who confirmed his status as world number one with six victories and record 12 month winnings of $2.5 million and Raymond Floyd, the 50-year-old whose competitive edge is as sharp today as it was when he won his first title 30 years ago in Florida.

Floyd dipped in and out of the US regular and senior Tours, becoming the first player to win on both in the same season, and took the Doral title in Florida just two weeks after fire destroyed his $1.7 million home. Floyd, like Sam Snead, has now won US Tour events in four decades, a feat that prompted Arnold Palmer to wire him with the succinct message: 'Older is better.'

Yet for sheer brilliance of performance Faldo was the golfer who operated on a different plateau, winning an emotional and dramatic third Open and fifth Major success tieing him with Seve Ballesteros, whose 1992 season, in contrast and despite two early wins, turned out to be as downbeat as his 1991 had been celebratory. Seve hopefully will come back.

Faldo plans to build over the next ten years on a solid foundation of proper preparation, hard work on the practice range and a new lighter approach to the business of winning tournaments encouraged by his reading of a book entitled: *Being Happy*. He certainly was in 1992, a year when his world

travels took him to Jamaica, southern Africa, Thailand, Japan, the United States, Dubai in the Middle East and seven countries in Europe on which Tour he set new prize-money records as well with a stroke average of 69.10 for 60 rounds.

In a year when Fred Couples, Nick Price and, more sentimentally, Tom Kite won their first Majors, Faldo won the Open at Muirfield, tied second in the USPGA, came fourth in the US Open - now his main target - and tied 13th at Augusta in the Masters. Over the past four years Faldo's consistency in the Majors, around which he builds his schedule each season Jack Nicklaus-style, has been phenomenal and in 1992 in those events that lay claim to being world golf's fifth Major he came joint second in the Players Championship, won the World Matchplay Championship title for a second time and picked up the Johnnie Walker World Championship in Jamaica after a great last day duel with Greg Norman, surely one of the game's unluckiest players.

In a year when Amsterdam-based international brewing company Heineken took over sponsorship of the World Cup and extended its global commitment to the sport by increasing its association with both the European and Australasian Tours, commentators debated whether or not golf should be included in the 1996 Olympics and, if it must, whether it should involve only top amateurs. Those who insist that for commercial reasons professionals need to be involved, will ensure that the argument -

pros or amateurs?- will rage on with only one thing agreed by everyone, namely that any move to turn Olympic golf into a carnival sport like basketball was at Barcelona with the so-called Dream Team is not the route to take, however much money it might make.

Golf had its own dream team in 1992: Captained by Mickey Walker and led by Laura Davies, the European women professionals invited the Americans to Dalmahoy and, in rain and wind, proved that just as Europe's Ryder Cup men no longer fear their American counterparts neither do the European women now freeze when confronting the LPGA superstars. It helped perhaps that six of the European side now play regularly in America but the impact of Europe's Solheim Cup win captured every golfer's imagination and will, hopefully, help the European Women's Tour with its stop-start schedule to establish itself more strongly over the next few years.

The Solheim professionals and the Great Britain and Ireland side which beat the Americans for the third time in four Curtis Cup matches, this time at Hoylake, ensured that women's golf hit the headlines for at least two weeks in 1992, but Floyd and especially Faldo were headline makers throughout another great year; a year when Ernie Els with six wins in South Africa established himself as a star of the future,

when Robert Allenby gave every indication that he could be Australia's next dominant golfer and Phil Mickelson, the left-hander who won a US Tour event at Tucson as an amateur in 1991, turned pro and promised much as America's newest star on a circuit which can, at year's end, boast 155 dollar prize-money millionaires 24 years after Arnold Palmer made the first million. In 1992 golf beat the recession and the professionals, whom Greg Norman (of all people) calls the luckiest sportsmen around because sponsors keep putting up more and more money for them to play for, produced superb performances in every corner of the globe - from the irrepressible Lee Trevino who once again won a hatful of tournaments and a million dollars on the US Senior Tour to Jamie Spence whose brilliant 12 under par 60 at Crans enabled him to come from 10 behind to capture his first European title. There was no Ryder Cup but 1992 was a year of records, a year of triumphs for some and disappointments for others, but a year to remember and a year when Nick Faldo established a seven point lead at the top of the world rankings and more than ever justified his status as a global superstar in the best Jack Nicklaus-Ben Hogan tradition.

RENTON LAIDLAW
Evening Standard, London
January 1993

INTRODUCTION

By Nick Edmund

Welcome to the first *Heineken World of Golf*. The idea of a golfing annual may not be a novel one but we are confident that you will find more than a hint of novelty in the style and presentation of this particular golf compendium. You will certainly find plenty of colour and excitement within its 224 pages for the Royal and Ancient game has become a hugely colourful and exciting sport: 1992 was a fine example and 1993 is sure to be equally enthralling. That, in the proverbial nutshell, is what this book is all about - capturing the style, reliving the drama and indulging in the unique wonder of golf.

The book's chosen title is the *Heineken World of Golf*, rather than, for instance, the Heineken Golf Year, because our intention is to celebrate the geography just as much as to record the immediate history of the game; it is no coincidence therefore that the third chapter charts golf's most truly international tournament, the World Cup and that the fourth is entitled 'Global Golf'. But I have just driven out of turn. Chapters One and Two come first and they set the scene by respectively looking back and reflecting on the highlights of the past year - suggesting how and why it might be remembered in years to come - and reviewing in detail the season's four Major championships.

So after 'Highlights', 'Grand Slam Golf' and 'World Cup Golf' we reach our 'Global Golf' chapter. This is the biggest section of the book and it includes reports, results and an array of striking photography from all the major men's and women's tours and tournaments around the world: matchplay golf, amateur golf, senior golf and team golf are all featured and hopefully you will find there to be a nice balance of statistical and analytical information. Chapter Five, '1993: A Year to Savour' comprises previews of all this season's big events including, of course, the eagerly awaited Ryder Cup match at The Belfry; and then the concluding section, 'Great Golf Courses of the World', which appears for no other purpose than to show off some of the game's finest and most unusual playgrounds.

Finally, as editor I would like to take this opportunity to thank one or two people and organisations without whom the project would have never got off the ground. Firstly, our sponsor, Heineken, whose enthusiasm for golf would seem to know no frontiers, and our highly professional publishers, Stanley Paul. Special thanks go to Rob Kelland, the designer of this book who has clearly done a tremendous job. I am indebted to Renton Laidlaw for providing the foreword, and to the directors of Allsport in whose premises (along with my living room) this book has largely been assembled; nor must I forget their staff (particularly Julie Kay and Andrew Reddington) and their legion of golf photographers, led by Dave Cannon, who have provided the vast majority of the book's two hundred pictures. Last, but by no means least, I thank my wife, Teresa for her treasured and constant support.

1992
A YEAR TO REMEMBER
....

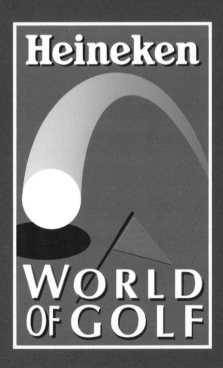

1992
A Year to Remember

1992 HIGHLIGHTS AND REFLECTIONS

· ·

One of the oldest sayings in the English language is, 'never judge a book by its cover'. I think I can speak on behalf of the principal photographer and designer if I say that we hope you will judge this book by its cover. Our intention has been to try and encapsulate in four striking pictures the essence of the world of golf as it passes from 1992 to 1993.

Maybe somewhere in 50 years time this first *Heineken World of Golf* will be plucked from a dusty bookshelf; if it is by an old-timer with a sound memory then hopefully when he or she glances at the front cover familiar images will instantly come flooding back: images of the world's major players in the midst of a golden age of golf. In particular, that sound memory might focus on a year when Fred Couples, an unassuming American with a strange habit of wheeling his arms over his head as if his shirts didn't fit properly, finally raised his arms in triumph at a Major championship; when a Spaniard, the most charismatic, mercurial golfer of the time, waded deep into the rough and couldn't seem to find a clear way out and the swashbuckling, all-guns blazing Australian they called the Great White Shark seemed - late in the year at least - to be on the verge of recapturing his best 'storming Norman' form. And probably the most

dominant image of all from that season will stare back: of a relentless, golfing colossus whom the old-timers of the day had begun to compare with the legendary Ben Hogan.

At the end of 1992 there was no doubt, not even a reasonable doubt as lawyers say, as to who was the best golfer in the world; but a third of the way through the year there was just a smidgen of doubt. Fred Couples, a man 'so laid back his eyes appear to be pointing permanently at the moon', as one journalist suggested, won the Masters in April to set the seal on an incredible run on form that had begun 10 months before at the 1991 US Open. During that period he dislodged Ian Woosnam from his number one world ranking position, (in addition to relieving him of his Masters green jacket) won six events, was runner-up three times and came third five times; in total he played in 25 tournaments and only failed to finish in the top six on five occasions. However, there were no further individual wins in 1992 for Couples (although he did successfully team up with Davis Love to capture November's World Cup of Golf for America) and his form for much of the latter half of the year was patchy.

Nick Faldo's form throughout 1992 was rarely anything short of 'awesome' - the word he himself adopted, tongue in cheek. What presently sets him apart from his contemporaries, or, if you like, what makes him the dominant golfer of his age, is that he alone seems able to tune and prime his form so that it has every chance of peaking at the year's big events; that is why his record in the Grand Slam championships over the past five years (he has never been out of the top 30 in 22 successive Majors) is vastly superior to any other of today's leading players. Faldo came 13th at Augusta and from the next event he entered in May until the European Open in September his sequence of finishes was 3rd, 2nd, 8th, 4th, 1st, 4th (the US Open), 3rd, 3rd, 1st (the Open), 1st, 2nd (the US PGA), 1st.

There were some similarities in the way that Couples won his first Major at Augusta and Faldo his fifth in the Open at Muirfield. Both, for instance, went into their final 18 holes having played three rounds in the 60s; both were three shots ahead when they 'turned for home' and both had the alarm bells ringing during those final nine holes - Couples when his ball seemed destined for Rae's Creek at the 12th and Faldo when he dropped three strokes in four holes from the 11th. But Lady Luck smiled on the American, for his ball suddenly stopped rolling downhill into the water, and she did on the tall Englishman when his main challenger, John Cook, missed a very short putt on the penultimate hole. But fortune, remember, smiles on the brave as well and the two displayed enormous courage in sticking to their task (in the case of Faldo by playing 'the best four holes of my life') and each was able to weather the storm.

Tom Kite also 'weathered the storm' in 1992 - quite literally - to win the US Open at Pebble Beach (his level par 72 in the final round was, given the conditions, arguably the round of the year) and in the season's fourth Major championship, the USPGA,

Zimbabwean Nick Price joined Couples and Kite as popular first-time Major winners. Our two other friends from the front cover, Seve Ballesteros and Greg Norman, didn't get so much as a sniff of Major glory in 1992, yet probably as much ink was spilt over their exploits during the year as over those of Kite and Price. The reason is simple enough: they remain the two most exciting players in the world of golf.

For the first few months of the year Fred Couples seemed invincible

For many avid followers of the sport the biggest disappointment of the mid to late 1980s was that these two great players and personalities hardly every clashed head to head, à la Nicklaus and Watson, in the big events. Their paths still rarely cross: the man from the Northern Hemisphere plays most of his golf in Europe and the man from the Southern Hemisphere plays most of his golf in America. Their moods and form were poles apart too in 1992. Norman started his year 'frustrated in February' (he 'threw away' the Australian Masters for a second year running and was then sidelined until April with a knee injury) but gradually the Great White Shark of old started to nibble his way back; then in September he devoured the Canadian Open and his final round of the year was a dazzling 63 in Jamaica; he didn't win that event because of you-know-who but declared, 'I'll be feeding off that round for a long time.' A typical shark comment. Seve's first tournament score of the year was a 65 in the Asian Classic in February; he won in Dubai the following week and again in Majorca a month later. Then suddenly his game disintegrated. He shot an 81 in the last round of the Masters; a 79 in the fourth round of the US Open; missed the cut at Muirfield and didn't even play in the USPGA at Bellerive. Can Seve find his way back out of that deep rough in 1993 and beyond? Only time will tell, of course, but just ask yourself, if you were lying badly in the rough and needed to play some magical Houdini-like recovery shot, who'd be your first choice to play the shot for you?

Today, Faldo, Couples, Ballesteros and Norman may be the major figures of the age, but Father Time will catch up with them one day (even if he seems to have given Ray Floyd an extended permit). In the year 2000, perhaps an appropriate collage of pictures to illustrate the great players of the world of golf will comprise images of South African Ernie Els, Australian Robert Allenby and American Phil Mickelson (mind you, the 'big hopes' for American golf 7 - 10 years ago were Bob Tway, Hal Sutton and Bobby Clampett!) There should also be space for Señor Olazabal on this hypothetical cover, although he will need to play much better over the next few years than he did in 1992. Els and Allenby were the two young players

Steven Richardson – Rainy days and missed cuts

who made the biggest impact last year. Els took the South African Tour by storm with six wins and Allenby overwhelmed a strong field to win a big event at Royal Melbourne, en route to heading the 1992 Australasian Order of Merit in his rookie season. It will be very interesting to see how they perform in 1993 and, equally, where they choose to play most of their golf in the years ahead. Will their paths cross frequently?

If Olazabal's year was a disappointing one (he actually won twice but at times appeared to be carrying the entire world on his shoulders) it was a far worse one for England's most promising young player in 1991, Steven Richardson. He had no victories at all in 1992 and missed the cut seven times on the European Tour. There were no wins either for Colin Montgomerie, although the

Their names are all appropriate: (top left) Montgomerie has just stormed the back nine at Pebble Beach; (top right) Cook can't stand the heat of leading the Open and (bottom) Price is just about to pay heavily for a blunder at the Sun City Million Dollar Challenge

Scot seemed to be challenging in almost every event he played in and in June came very close to winning the US Open. 'Monty' actually thought he had won at Pebble Beach when he holed out for a par on the 18th green with the wind seemingly poised to blow away the hopes of all those still out on the course. John Cook is a second player who must have thought a first Major championship win was only moments away as he walked onto Muirfield's 17th green in the final round of the Open. But Cook proceeded to take three bites at the cherry: 'There goes a hundred thousand bucks', was the immortal cry of Al Waltrous in 1927 when his chances of winning the Open were scuppered at the 71st hole (a victim of Bobby Jones' miracle shot at Lytham): Cook might have wished to add at least one more zero for inflation to that number. A million dollars, however, is precisely the sum that

Their Cups runneth over: joyous scenes as Great Britain and Ireland triumph in the Curtis Cup and (below) Europe defeat the United States in the Solheim Cup

Nick Price kissed good-bye to when in a fit of temper he elected not to sign, or rather erased his signature after signing, his score card at the Sun City Million Dollar Challenge last December. Price completed his third round tied for the lead - or so he thought - but then discovered that he was to be penalised two strokes for moving an advertising hoarding that had obstructed his view of the flag at the 11th hole.

Coincidentally, Nick Faldo was also disqualified after the third round at Sun City: not the result of any temper tantrum, but for the elementary mistake of signing for an incorrectly entered score, after which all David Frost needed to do was to keep his head down, play conservatively, sign his name properly and pick up a million dollar cheque. All in all, a hard day at the office.

Bophuthatswana and million dollar pay days must have seemed light years away for the participants at Hoylake in the 27th Curtis Cup match in June. But whereas David Frost won his incredulous sum of money playing at a canter on the final day, the amateur women of Great Britain and Ireland fought their counterparts from America tooth and nail all the way to the final green of the final match. There were euphoric scenes when the home side triumphed - just as there were four months later at Dalmahoy when the European women professionals defeated America in the 2nd Solheim Cup match. This win was widely regarded as 'the achievement of the year'. Europe's captain, Mickey Walker, even went so far as to describe it as 'one of the greatest sporting achievements of the century'. Walker is naturally biased but she probably wasn't all that far wide of the mark: only two years earlier at Lake Nona in the inaugural Solheim Cup encounter the gap in class between the standard of women's play in Europe and America had seemed as wide as the Grand Canyon; now suddenly since Edinburgh last Autumn it looks no wider than the width of the Swilcan Burn.

The Solheim Cup success (as with the Curtis Cup) was clearly very much a team effort but there were two players on either side who had exceptional individual seasons in 1992. Sweden's Helen Alfredsson won twice in Europe and once in Japan; she also came close to winning three times in

America where she was named LPGA Rookie of the Year and partnered Lotte Neumann to win the Sunrise World Team Cup for Sweden. Britain's Laura Davies enjoyed only a modest year in America but won three events on the WPGE Tour, comfortably collected the Order of Merit title and was unquestionably the star performer (and inspiration of the European side) at Dalmahoy. Patty Sheehan and Dottie Mochrie

Dottie Mochrie, the leading player on the 1992 LPGA Tour

were the two Americans with most to celebrate in 1992: Mochrie won four LPGA tournaments (including a first Major) and was Leading Moneywinner while Sheehan became the first ever player to achieve the women's US-British Open double.

Switching sexes and continents, towards the end of the year Steve Elkington (our man on the back cover) grabbed the biggest prize of the Australasian season when he won the Heineken Australian Open in Sydney, his first ever major win in his home country and Jumbo Ozaki ended his season having once again dominated the Japanese Tour. He won six tournaments in 1992, the same number

(Top left)
Caddieing the
Californian way
(top right)
Caddieing the
Jamaican way
(bottom left)
Anders
Forsbrand, the
not-so-ice-cool
Swede and
(bottom right)
Craig Stadler,
the
not-so-chuffed
walrus

(Left) Greg
Norman ended
1992 with his
confidence
sky-high after
scoring a
brilliant 63 in
Jamaica; by
contrast Seve
Ballesteros
(inset)
appeared to
have lost
his way

as Nick Faldo and Ernie Els but remains a parochial champion. Luring Jumbo out of Japan has proved only marginally easier over the years than guiding a camel through the eye of a needle: he didn't, for instance, travel to Jamaica at the end of the year for the Johnnie Walker World Championship - not that one imagines he could have played sufficiently well to challenge the charging Greg Norman and the all-conquering Nick Faldo, who finished nine strokes ahead of the rest of the field, although Jumbo would surely have beaten Seve Ballesteros who propped up the entire cast.

A charging Norman, an all-conquering Faldo and a slumping Seve: we seem to have come full circle. So, 1993 beckons and dare we suggest a quick wager on Nick Faldo to win the Grand Slam? Surely not. Not even Ben Hogan could achieve that... but you can bet your life that it won't be for the want of trying.

Golden days for
Nick Faldo –
a latter-day
Ben Hogan?

THE SONY RANKINGS

31ST · DECEMBER · 1992

Position	Player	Circuit	Points
1	Nick Faldo	Eur	23.54
2	Fred Couples	USA	16.27
3	Ian Woosnam	Eur	13.14
4	José-Maria Olazabal	Eur	12.87
5	Greg Norman	ANZ	12.63
6	Bernhard Langer	Eur	12.44
7	John Cook	USA	11.68
8	Nick Price	Afr	11.51
9	Paul Azinger	USA	10.83
10	Davis Love III	USA	10.75
11	Tom Kite	USA	10.17
12	Mark O'Meara	USA	9.49
13	Seve Ballesteros	Eur	9.44
14	Raymond Floyd	USA	9.35
15	Masashi Ozaki	Jpn	9.17
16	Corey Pavin	USA	8.91
17	Bruce Lietzke	USA	8.45
18	Steve Elkington	ANZ	7.77
19	Mark McNulty	Afr	7.53
20	Colin Montgomerie	Eur	7.48
21	Payne Stewart	USA	7.01
22	Craig Parry	ANZ	6.95
23	Rodger Davis	ANZ	6.64
24	Ian Baker-Finch	ANZ	6.63
25	Chip Beck	USA	6.63
26	David Frost	Afr	6.52
27	Jeff Sluman	USA	6.50
28	Tony Johnstone	Afr	6.39
29	Sandy Lyle	Eur	6.29
30	Tom Watson	USA	6.05
31	Lanny Wadkins	USA	5.87
32	Peter Senior	ANZ	5.78
33	Brad Faxon	USA	5.57
34	Steve Pate	USA	5.57
35	Ronan Rafferty	Eur	5.57
36=	Eduardo Romero	SAm	5.41
36=	Craig Stadler	USA	5.41
38	Vijay Singh	Asa	5.35
39	Anders Forsbrand	Eur	5.20
40	Ernie Els	Afr	5.16
41	Gene Sauers	USA	5.07
42	Jim Gallagher Jnr	USA	5.04
43	Dan Forsman	USA	5.01
44	Mark Brooks	USA	4.92
45	Jose Rivero	Eur	4.86
46	Duffy Waldorf	USA	4.85
47	Naomichi Ozaki	Jpn	4.80
48	Mark Calcavecchia	USA	4.77
49	Hale Irwin	USA	4.76
50	John Huston	USA	4.64
51	Ben Crenshaw	USA	4.60
52	Steven Richardson	Eur	4.56
53	Larry Mize	USA	4.55
54	David Edwards	USA	4.54
55	David Feherty	Eur	4.48
56	Frank Nobilo	ANZ	4.43
57	Mark James	Eur	4.37
58	Jay Haas	USA	4.33
59	David Gilford	Eur	4.29
60	Barry Lane	Eur	4.29
61	Tom Purtzer	USA	4.23
62	Billy Andrade	USA	4.20
63	John Daly	USA	4.20
64	Rocco Mediate	USA	4.18

Ernie Els began 1992 in 418th position in the Sony Rankings – by the end of the year he had climbed to number 40. (Opposite page) Nick Faldo established a record points total in 1992 and a huge lead over Fred Couples at the top

THE MAJORS

THE US MASTERS
THE US OPEN
THE OPEN
THE USPGA

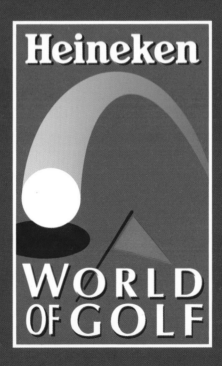

THE US MASTERS

THE US MASTERS

ROLL · OF · HONOUR

The 'European Masters'

1934	Horton Smith	1966	* Jack Nicklaus	
1935	* Gene Sarazen	1967	Gay Brewer	
1936	Horton Smith	1968	Bob Goalby	
1937	Byron Nelson	1969	George Archer	
1938	Henry Picard	1970	* Billy Casper	
1939	Ralph Guldahl	1971	Charles Coody	
1940	Jimmy Demaret	1972	Jack Nicklaus	
1941	Craig Wood	1973	Tommy Aaron	
1942	* Byron Nelson	1974	Gary Player	
1943-5	No championships played	1975	Jack Nicklaus	
1946	Herman Keiser	1976	Ray Floyd	
1947	Jimmy Demaret	1977	Tom Watson	
1948	Claude Harmon	1978	Gary Player	
1949	Sam Snead	1979	* Fuzzy Zoeller	
1950	Jimmy Demaret	1980	Seve Ballesteros	
1951	Ben Hogan	1981	Tom Watson	
1952	Sam Snead	1982	* Craig Stadler	
1953	Ben Hogan	1983	Seve Ballesteros	
1954	* Sam Snead	1984	Ben Crenshaw	
1955	Cary Middlecoff	1985	Bernhard Langer	
1956	Jack Burke	1986	Jack Nicklaus	
1957	Doug Ford	1987	* Larry Mize	
1958	Arnold Palmer	1988	Sandy Lyle	
1959	Art Wall	1989	* Nick Faldo	
1960	Arnold Palmer	1990	* Nick Faldo	
1961	Gary Player	1991	Ian Woosnam	
1962	* Arnold Palmer	1992	Fred Couples	
1963	Jack Nicklaus			
1964	Arnold Palmer		* Winner in play-off.	
1965	Jack Nicklaus			

· HIGHLIGHTS ·

Most wins:
  6 Jack Nicklaus
  4 Arnold Palmer
Most times runner-up:
  4 Ben Hogan
     Tom Weiskopf
     Jack Nicklaus
Biggest margin of victory:
  9 Jack Nicklaus (1965)
Lowest winning total:
  271 Jack Nicklaus (1965)
       Ray Floyd (1976)
Lowest single round:
  63 Nick Price (1986)
Lowest final round by winner:
  64 Gary Player (1978)
Oldest champion:
     Jack Nicklaus,
     aged 46 (1986)
Youngest champion:
     Severiano Ballesteros,
     aged 23 (1980)

THE 1992 US MASTERS

Were those handsome features supported by a glass jaw?
Or could Fred Couples prove the doubters wrong?
Augusta would reveal all.

Each one of us, somewhere along the line has said something we regret. How about this comment from 1973 Open Champion, Tom Weiskopf, a few years back: 'Great talent Fred Couples, but no goals in life, not one.' To be fair to Weiskopf he only uttered in public what many people had whispered privately; moreover until approximately half way through 1991 Couples' career path seemed to be heading ominously in the direction of that infamous golfing cul-de-sac called 'unfulfilled potential'.

From the moment Fred Couples birdied the final hole of the 1991 US Open Championship to finish in third place behind Payne Stewart and Scott Simpson he seemed to become a changed man: still laid-back, still unassuming, but an inspired golfer. In the period between that US Open at Hazeltine and his date with destiny at Augusta Couples played consistently better golf than anyone on earth. Two weeks after the US Open he comfortably won the Federal Express St. Jude Classic and followed it with a third place in the prestigious Western Open. He challenged strongly in the Open Championship at Royal Birkdale - again finishing third - and eventually went on to record the lowest aggregate total for the year's four Major championships. He won the BC Open in September and ended

the season with the PGA Tour's lowest scoring average; the icing on his 1991 cake came with a December victory in the inaugural Johnnie Walker World Championship in Jamaica.

Not only was it happy Christmas for Fred, it was also a glorious New Year as his golf became even more devastating. In the five US tournaments he entered leading up to the Masters, Couples had two wins and two second places, and his combined score for those five events was an extraordinary 71 under par. On Saturdays he was especially impressive. How do rounds of 64 - 69 - 65 - 63 - 63 sound?! It was shades of Johnny Miller in the mid 1970s. Little wonder then that as the world's golfing elite assembled for the first Major of 1992 the rest of the cast were in awe of the popular American. Nick Faldo summed it up in his own inimitable way when he said of the favourite, 'He's so hot, he should be wearing asbestos underpants.'

In stark contrast to all this was the mood of the defending champion, Ian Woosnam. 'I am playing like a 24 handicapper' the Welshman told a disbelieving press (some of whom had heard rumours of a 64 during practice). 'It's going to be a short week,' he added.

Two-time champion Faldo was a little more confident about his prospects while

Spanish hopes were high with both Ballesteros and Olazabal having won twice already on the European Tour. Other potential threats to the all conquering Couples? There was much talk on the eve of the tournament about the quality and depth of the Australian challenge and, although Greg Norman was only appearing courtesy of a last minute invitation, much was expected of Messrs. Elkington, already a winner on the 1992 US Tour, Baker-Finch, the reigning Open Champion and the Australian Masters

Imagine a green jacket on top of this tee-shirt!
Ian Woosnam made a spirited defence despite his
indifferent form

winner Craig Parry - and for three days at least they didn't disappoint. Yet even if Couples couldn't pull it off there was a strong feeling that after an unprecedented run of foreign successes, 1992, the five hundredth anniversary of Columbus' voyage, was going to herald an American victory.

When eagerly awaited Thursday finally came by far the biggest (and noisiest) gallery was the one following John Daly. It was of course 'Long John's' first Major appearance since his astonishing performance in the USPGA at Crooked Stick. Well, the whooping and hollering 'You're the Man' brigade got precisely what they came for as Daly proceeded to pound the ball as only he can; he hit it so hard and so far that the famous Augusta pines and dogwoods began to tremble. But it was two other USPGA Champions, Lanny Wadkins and Jeff Sluman, who were holing all the putts. Both scored 65s in the first round and Sluman's seven under par round included a hole in one at the 4th, the first ever at that hole in the Masters. At the end of the day they led by one stroke from fellow American Jodie Mudd. No fewer than eighteen players achieved sub 70 rounds and a total of thirty-five players scored under par. Couples opened his account with a 69, as to his (but nobody else's) amazement did Ian Woosnam. Among others on that mark were 'old campaigners' Jack Nicklaus and the in-form Ray Floyd, Craig Parry and Bernhard Langer. Greg Norman had a 70 while Nick Faldo took 71, the same score as John Daly. As for Spanish eyes they were anything but smiling on Thursday evening for posted against the names Ballesteros and Olazabal were the scores 75 and 76. A sunken Armada.

Some phenomenal golf was played on the second day at Augusta last year, and most of it by Craig Parry, Ian Woosnam and Fred

Couples; between them they shared no fewer than twenty-three birdies: Parry and Woosnam with seven a piece in their 66s and Couples with nine in a roller-coaster 67. They didn't exactly spread-eagle the field but with the first round leaders all falling by the wayside (Sluman 74, Wadkins 75 and Mudd 78) it did surge them to the front of the pack. The evergreen, 49-year-old Ray Floyd, a winner in 1976 and runner-up to Faldo in 1990, clung doggedly to the leaders' coat-tails adding a 68 to his first round 69. Within five strokes of the lead were a total of six overseas players, including the four fancied Australians, though not Nick Faldo who could only manage a modest 72. But the top of the leader board at the half way stage read: 135 Parry and Woosnam; 136 Couples; 137 Floyd and Schulz. No one could remember the last time a twenty-four handicapper had led the Masters. A huge smile lit up Woosnam's face when he holed a twenty foot putt on the 18th green for his 66 - the same score he had managed in the second round twelve months earlier. Even he now accepted that he was perfectly placed to win a second green jacket, nor had it escaped anyone's notice that such a feat would make it five in a row for British golfers. (I wonder what odds you could have got on that happening ten years ago!)

Talk about 'whether' became talk about 'weather' by mid afternoon on Saturday. None of the early starters made any significant progress, or to use golfing parlance, 'nobody was shooting the lights out'. Nick Price (67), Nick Faldo (68) and Ian Baker-Finch (68) did haul themselves up the leader board, but the 1992 Masters was developing into an intriguing four-way contest between Parry, Woosnam, Couples and Floyd. And what contrasting two balls they made! Five-foot-four Woosnam and

five-foot-six Parry were the last to tee off on Saturday and playing directly ahead of the 'popeye pairing' were the duo dubbed 'Butch Cassidy and the Sun Dance Kid' after their heroic performances together during the 1991 Ryder Cup at Kiawah Island. (If anyone was going to 'shoot the lights out' it was surely them?)

The overseas pair made the first move but no sooner had they started to trade birdies with one another than the dreaded Georgian thunderclouds appeared overhead. A three-hour delay was the result and when the players returned to the course Woosnam (and initially Parry) had lost the Midas touch. It brought back memories of Tony Jacklin in 1970 at St. Andrews. Then, as now, the British golfer was defending his first Major title; he was leading, playing outrageously well but was halted in his tracks by a tempest-induced stoppage and then, as now, a different golfer emerged on resumption. 'What did you do during the three-hour delay?' somebody asked before they teed off again. 'I had ten pints,' cracked Woosnam. He hadn't of course but for the next half hour he proceeded, as Ian Wooldridge wryly remarked in *The Mail On Sunday*, 'To play like a man who'd drunk them with double whisky chasers.' Both Parry and Woosnam double bogeyed their first hole (the 4th) and although the Australian soon recovered his composure, Woosnam continued to play like the 24 handicapper he'd been promising; in the space of seven holes five shots were frittered away.

The interruption didn't halt the flow of birdies from either Floyd or Couples, although they did mix some magnificent stroke play with the occasional aberration, and Parry putted his way back to the top of the leader board. It wasn't quite possible to

Aussies at Augusta: Craig Parry (main picture) led after 54 holes while Greg Norman and Ian Baker-Finch, (who would both love to add a Masters title to the Open Championships they won in 1986 and 1991 respectively) finished tied for 6th

complete the third round on Saturday but after the final pairings had managed to do so early on the Sunday morning Parry (12 under par) held a one stroke advantage over Couples and led Floyd by two. Baker-Finch was three behind his compatriate and Woosnam, thanks to two courageous birdies at the end of his round, had got himself back to eight under par.

According to Rodger Davis, 'Not one in

would look pretty impressive in anyone's wardrobe. After two holes of the final round Parry was three in front of his playing partner Couples, the 'super-hot' pre-tournament favourite. Throughout the week he had putted superbly ; the holes, it seemed, were the size of buckets whenever Parry stood over a six-foot putt. Then suddenly he missed one. Then another, then another - three 3-putts came in succession

ten (among the partisan Augusta galleries) had ever heard of Craig Parry.' Yet the stocky Australian was on the verge of an historic Australian-US Masters double, something Greg Norman has never been able to achieve. A little garish perhaps, but a gold blazer from Huntingdale and a green one from Augusta

and by the time they reached the turn, it was Parry who trailed Couples by three.

Super-cool Fred wasn't doing anything spectacular, in fact he was playing a very un-Couples-like game - percentage golf. With Parry going from bad to worse (he eventually stumbled his way to a closing 78) it was

It missed by a whisker: Ray Floyd (left) just fails to birdie the 16th hole on Sunday. (Right) Fred Couples at the 12th playing from the spot where Sir Isaac Newton's theory went up in smoke

On his way: Couples drives at the 72nd hole

ironic that the veteran Floyd, the man acclaimed as Couples' mentor, the man said to be responsible for turning his career around, should now be his closest challenger. Floyd battled away gainfully as only Floyd can but despite pitching in for a magnificent birdie at the 14th and then so nearly holing putts for a three at the 15th and a two at the 16th the stage was set fair for Couples to march triumphantly to his first Major title. Of course the one thing Couples never did was march. From his outward demeanour, and the way he casually strolled the velvet fairways, Fred might as well have been playing a friendly game with his buddies.

Inside however, his stomach must have been churning, particularly when his poorly struck tee shot to the notorious par three 12th appeared to be tumbling downhill into the water that fronts the green. But it seems Fred was destined to win and 'gravity hiccupped', as one commentator put it. Fred survived the scare and went on to play the final six holes in one under par for a two stroke victory. America hailed its first home-grown champion since Larry Mize in '87 - no extra time or miracle strokes were required on this occasion - just a good old fashioned case of the cream rising to the top. Funny how it usually does, down in Good Old Georgia.

1992 US MASTERS

FINAL · SCORES

Major and minor – Ian Woosnam presents Fred Couples with his first green jacket

F Couples	69	67	69	70	275	$270,000
R Floyd	69	68	69	71	277	162,000
C Pavin	72	71	68	67	278	102,000
J Sluman	65	74	70	71	280	66,000
M O'Meara	74	67	69	70	280	66,000
S Pate	73	71	70	67	281	43,829
N Henke	70	71	70	70	281	43,829
I Baker-Finch	70	69	68	74	281	43,829
N Price	70	71	67	73	281	43,829
G Norman	70	70	73	68	281	43,829
L Mize	73	69	71	68	281	43,829
T Schulz	68	69	72	72	281	43,829
D Pruitt	75	68	70	69	282	26,500
W Grady	68	75	71	68	282	26,500
S Simpson	70	71	71	70	282	26,500
B Leitzke	69	72	68	73	282	26,500
N Faldo	71	72	68	71	282	26,500
C Parry	69	66	69	78	282	26,500
B R Brown	70	74	70	69	283	17,550
A Magee	73	70	70	70	283	17,550
M Hulbert	68	74	71	70	283	17,550
I Woosnam	69	66	73	75	283	17,550
F Zoeller	71	70	73	69	283	17,550
J Daly	71	71	73	68	283	17,550
B Fleisher	73	70	72	69	284	11,467
J Huston	69	73	73	69	284	11,467
C Stadler	70	71	70	73	284	11,467
J Gallagher Jnr	74	68	71	71	284	11,467
D Love III	68	72	72	72	284	11,467
D A Weibring	71	68	72	73	284	11,467
B Langer	69	73	69	74	285	8,717
B Faxon	71	71	69	74	285	8,717
S Richardson	69	75	70	71	285	8,717
C Strange	73	72	71	69	285	8,717
P Azinger	70	73	70	72	285	8,717
M Calcavecchia	73	72	75	65	285	8,717
C Montgomerie	72	71	73	70	286	6,800
S Elkington	69	71	74	72	286	6,800
M McCumber	72	70	76	68	286	6,800
S Lyle	72	69	70	75	286	6,800
R Mediate	70	73	70	73	286	6,800
B Gilder	72	71	73	71	287	5,450
J Nicklaus	69	75	69	74	287	5,450
J M Olazabal	76	69	72	70	287	5,450
B Mayfair	71	71	72	73	287	5,450
B Crenshaw	72	71	71	74	288	4,700
H Irwin	72	70	72	75	289	4,400
B McCallister	71	71	76	72	290	3,933
L Wadkins	65	75	76	74	290	3,933
T Watson	73	70	76	71	290	3,933
G Archer	74	69	76	72	291	3,700
F Allem	69	71	78	74	292	3,550
D Feherty	73	72	77	70	292	3,550
B Andrade	73	71	73	76	293	3,440
J Cook	72	73	71	77	293	3,440
L Janzen	74	71	74	74	293	3,440
T Aaron	76	69	77	71	293	3,440
D Peoples	73	71	72	77	293	3,440
M Zerman*	70	71	76	77	294	Am.
S Ballesteros	75	68	70	81	294	3,300
P Jacobsen	72	70	77	76	295	3,300
T Purtzer	76	69	75	75	295	3,300
R Davis	77	68	77	79	301	3,200

* Denotes amateur

THE FIRST CADILLACS OF SPRING

A Commentary by Lauren St John

Sometimes it seems as if neither spring nor the golf season can begin until the first Cadillac has pulled into Magnolia Lane at Augusta National Golf Club, home of the US Masters, the first spectators have filtered out into the emerald perfection of the fairways, the first ball has found a watery grave in Rae's Creek and the first shot has been struck in earnest.

It is almost as though everything that comes before the Masters, the first Major championship of the year, is nothing more than preparation for what is to come. As if the long winter days and early season events have been devoted solely to the honing of those special skills which help a player to survive the mental and physical endurance test that is Augusta. For example, Seve Ballesteros took 18 inches off his backswing to enable him to control the ball more at the Masters before winning his first green jacket in 1980, and he played with a draw for four months at the start of 1992, just because he felt that a right-to-left shot was the key to reaching the par fives in two.

'It is the only golf course that I've ever been to where you start choking before you reach the clubhouse,' says Gary Player with a grin. He has won there three times and loves it. 'If there's a golf course like this in heaven, I hope I'm the head pro.'

'This is where the golf world gathers - a special place set aside for beauty and springtime,' Deane Beman, the US PGA Tour Commissioner, once said. 'You only see it, and remember it, as it exists in this one most beautiful week of the year.'

Augusta's aesthetic appeal is part of her fatal charm. When Bobby Jones first came to Georgia and saw what was to become his magnificent 'Cathedral in the Pines', it was a nursery, dominated by great pine forests and oak trees and interspersed with brilliant splashes of fuchsia pinks, white and scarlet azalea and dogwood. Jones chose to work with the land, rather than impose his will on it. Inspired by St Andrews, he created huge, undulating greens, which place such a premium on approach shot strategy and accuracy, that when Jack Nicklaus is preparing for the Masters he likes to stand on the putting surface, look back up the fairway and calculate his angle of attack like a chess-master.

These greens are the key to Augusta, and are so fast and so treacherous that it is said that when Byron Nelson hit a near perfect iron shot into the par three 16th hole, the ball bounced against the flag stick a foot above the hole and rebounded into the water. Even Ballesteros, one of the world's most gifted putters when he is playing well and a man who rehearsed for his Masters victories by practising his putting on the slick, unpredictable sands of Pedrena Beach, near his home in Spain, has four-putted the 16th. Asked what happened, he said simply: 'Well, I miss the putt, I miss the putt, I miss the putt, I make the putt.'

Experience means everything at the Masters, not only because it is the only Major championship that is played at a permanent venue, but also because many of Augusta's ambiguities and trouble spots are hidden from view. 'Deferred danger', 1984 Champion Ben Crenshaw calls it. In other words, it provokes thought. A player can't just stand on the tee and say to himself: 'There's rough on both sides and a bunker on the right. I'll take an iron off the tee.' He has to pit his wits against the course, to imagine where the danger might lurk, to consider his options and then to plot his way carefully from tee to green.

'Of all the courses in the world,' says Australian David Graham, 'Augusta National places the most emphasis on strategy and is the best example of what a Major is all about. Every shot here offers an option. That's the key. You've always got a safe side of the fairway or green to aim at, where you know you'll find your ball sitting on short grass. But from those safe spots you are not, by any means, guaranteed a par. From the wrong side of the fairways, you have much tougher approaches and then from the safe sides of the greens, you put enormous pressure on your putter. Caution here is an invitation to make bogeys.'

Nowhere is the mettle of a champion put to greater test than on Augusta's revered back nine holes. Curtis Strange (1985) and Seve Ballesteros (1986) are just two of the many great golfers who have seen their hopes drown in Rae's Creek. But for every tale of torment and terror at Augusta, there is one of hope and inspiration. Player once sat beside President Eisenhower in the Masters room at Augusta National and watched Arnold Palmer fail to get up and down from a plugged lie at the 72nd hole of the 1961 Masters to hand him the green jacket. 'I said to my wife: We're not going to lose. Arnold's not going to par the hole. We can still beat him. Because, you see, strange things happen in golf. And he played the shot the wrong way, you could see that on the television.'

Of all the shots that have swelled Masters lore, none is greater than Gene Sarazen's albatross in 1935. His caddie Stovepipe tried to talk him into taking a three-wood, but he was adamant that it was a 'turf-rider' or four-wood. 'The moment I hit it, I felt something in my bones. Walter Hagen was playing with me and Jones was watching beside the green. The sun was going down. I wasn't sure it had gone in the hole until I saw all 21 people jumping up and down.'

These stories of poetic justice and injustice are as much a part of Augusta's appeal as her sublime layout, her spacious and immaculate trimmed fairways, her whispering pines, her smooth, shining greens, her fragrant, jasmine-scented air and her vivid floral displays. As the writer John Updike said: 'The only difference at Augusta is that the divots tear loose on dotted lines.'

The overall effect is one of uninterrupted harmony, and there is nothing at the Masters to dispel that. Among the idiosyncrasies of the club's hierarchy is the strict enforcement of a colour-coding system, which means that everything from the dustbins to the sandwich wrapping paper is in the required shade of bottle green, sunshine yellow or white. Flowers that fail to bloom are replaced by artificial ones and the lakes are dyed blue. Tickets for the main event cannot be begged, borrowed or stolen, but are handed down from generation to generation, like heirlooms, so that even members of the gallery give the impression of being carefully chosen for visual impact.

But it is for these reasons as much as any that Augusta National has so endeared herself to us. They explain why it is that our memories of past championships there are sweeter and more colourful than those of any other tournament, why the greatest players always come to the fore there, and why it is that springtime only begins on the opening day of the US Masters.

THE US OPEN

THE US OPEN

ROLL · OF · HONOUR

1895	Horace Rawlins	1938	Ralph Guldahl	1983	Larry Nelson
1896	James Foulis	1939	* Byron Nelson	1984	* Fuzzy Zoeller
1897	Joe Lloyd	1940	* Lawson Little	1985	Andy North
1898	Fred Herd	1941	Craig Wood	1986	Ray Floyd
1899	Willie Smith	1942-5	No championships played	1987	Scott Simpson
1900	Harry Vardon	1946	* Lloyd Mangrum	1988	* Curtis Strange
1901	* Willie Anderson	1947	* Lew Worsham	1989	Curtis Strange
1902	Laurie Auchterlonie	1948	Ben Hogan	1990	* Hale Irwin
1903	* Willie Anderson	1949	Cary Middlecoff	1991	* Payne Stewart
1904	Willie Anderson	1950	* Ben Hogan	1992	Tom Kite
1905	Willie Anderson	1951	Ben Hogan		
1906	Alex Smith	1952	Julius Boros		
1907	Alex Ross	1953	Ben Hogan	* Winner in play-off.
1908	* Fred McLeod	1954	Ed Furgol		
1909	George Sargent	1955	* Jack Fleck		
1910	* Alex Smith	1956	Cary Middlecoff		
1911	* John McDermott	1957	* Dick Mayer	· HIGHLIGHTS ·
1912	John McDermott	1958	Tommy Bolt		
1913	* Francis Ouimet	1959	Billy Casper	**Most wins:**
1914	Walter Hagen	1960	Arnold Palmer	4 Willie Anderson
1915	Jerome Travers	1961	Gene Littler	Bobby Jones
1916	Charles Evans, Jr	1962	* Jack Nicklaus	Ben Hogan
1917-18	No championships played	1963	* Julius Boros	Jack Nicklaus
1919	* Walter Hagen	1964	Ken Venturi	**Most times runner-up:**
1920	Edward Ray	1965	* Gary Player	4 Bobby Jones
1921	James M. Barnes	1966	* Billy Casper	Sam Snead
1922	Gene Sarazen	1967	Jack Nicklaus	Arnold Palmer
1923	* Robert T. Jones	1968	Lee Trevino	Jack Nicklaus
1924	Cyril Walker	1969	Orville Moody	**Biggest margin of victory:**
1925	* W. MacFarlane	1970	Tony Jacklin	9 Willie Smith (1899)
1926	Robert T. Jones	1971	* Lee Trevino	Jim Barnes (1921)
1927	* Tommy Armour	1972	Jack Nicklaus	**Lowest winning total:**
1928	* Johnny Farrell	1973	Johnny Miller	272 Jack Nicklaus (1980)
1929	Robert T. Jones	1974	Hale Irwin	**Lowest single round:**
1930	Robert T. Jones	1975	* Lou Graham	63 Johnny Miller (1973)
1931	* Billy Burke	1976	Jerry Pate	Tom Weiskopf (1980)
1932	Gene Sarazen	1977	Hubert Green	Jack Nicklaus (1980)
1933	Johnny Goodman	1978	Andy North	**Lowest final round by winner:**
1934	Olin Dutra	1979	Hale Irwin	63 Johnny Miller (1973)
1935	Sam Parks, Jr	1980	Jack Nicklaus	**Oldest champion:**
1936	Tony Manero	1981	David Graham	Hale Irwin, aged 45 (1990)
1937	Ralph Guldahl	1982	Tom Watson	**Youngest champion:**
				Johnny McDermott,
				aged 19 (1911)

THE 1992 US OPEN

· ·

When beauty becomes beast only the bravest survive; the US Open at Pebble Beach produced an enthralling finish and a worthy champion

The setting is the Californian coast, 120 miles south of San Francisco. 'It's momentum, it's confidence, it's like a wave. You just have to catch one and ride it out and enjoy it while it lasts. I've been on a wave like that before. And I'm out there looking to catch another one. I'm just paddling around, waiting for another one to come in.' The words of a

Defending champion Payne Stewart couldn't rediscover his magical touch at Pebble Beach

local surf bum perhaps? We mustn't describe the sartorial 1991 US Open Champion as such. Payne Stewart was a man desperately seeking something on the eve of his title defence. Without a win in 1992, not even the majestic seascapes of the Monterey peninsula could inspire the star-spangled Stewart, and he was one player who never really challenged in what turned out to be a most extraordinary championship.

'Majestic' really is the word to describe Pebble Beach and its surrounds. 'The finest meeting of land and sea in the world' in the judgement of Robert Louis Stevenson. As for the course itself it presents, 'an epic of biblical dimensions' according to an American golf magazine. Pebble Beach has also been christened 'the St. Andrews of America' on account of the fact that it is (a) revered the world over, (b) beside the sea (one hesitates to say a links) and (c) open to the public (at $200 a round!). A comparison with Turnberry in fact is probably more appropriate - although most observers consider Pebble Beach's setting to be far more spectacular - because both great courses will be forever linked with the titanic Nicklaus v Watson battles of 1977 and 1982.

Nicklaus and Watson were back at Pebble Beach in June 1992. Jack was telling everybody that 'experience' was the key to unlocking Pebble Beach, and that because a regular PGA Tour event is annually staged on the famous course, the more seasoned American players enjoyed a distinct advantage. It was therefore ironic that at one point on Sunday Nicklaus, wearing his television commentator's hat, should be telling all and sundry that a 28-year-old, debut-making Scotsman had just captured his country's national championship.

Greg Norman and Ben Crenshaw hadn't qualified for the US Open, although it was a star-studded field nonetheless that gathered for the 92nd US Open Championship. The first of the seasoned campaigners to blaze an early trail at Pebble Beach was Curtis Strange. The champion of 1988 and 1989, but without a victory of any sort since, opened with a sparkling 67. Strange made his score by playing the 10th to the 15th holes in five under par. It wasn't however quite good enough for a first round lead as the even more seasoned Gil Morgan managed a six under par 66. Nor was Strange's back nine

birdie blitz the most scintillating sequence of the day: that achievement belonged to Andrew Dillard. Hardly anyone had heard of Dillard before the championship, indeed he was such an outsider that he had spent much of the early summer playing in numerous qualifying rounds just to earn a place at Pebble Beach. Well, he made the most of his opportunity by beginning birdie - birdie - birdie - birdie - birdie - birdie - six in a row from the first! Nobody had started a round like that in a Major championship since Greg Norman's famous final round onslaught at Troon in the 1989 Open. Dillard eventually returned a 68 to earn a share of third place with Steve Pate and the recently turned professional, Phil Mickelson. Of the overseas challengers, Nick Faldo and Colin Montgomerie led the way with two under par rounds of 70, one better than Sweden's Anders Forsbrand (who like Montgomerie was making an impressive first US Open appearance) and Seve Ballesteros. Many people were predicting, or at least hoping,

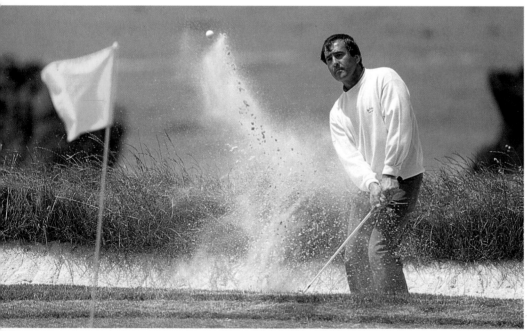

Seve and the sands of time: a first US Open title remains elusive for Ballesteros

that the Spaniard could be the man to beat at Pebble Beach, for if there is one US Open course made for his game it is surely this one. 'The Spanish were the first to discover Monterey' his supporters kept reminding him. Unfortunately Seve was having a little more trouble discovering his form.

Forty-five-year-old Gil Morgan was having no problem whatsoever. Doctor

Wayne Grady, whose 66 was once again the lowest score of the day. Forsbrand joined Montgomerie to lead the European challenge as Faldo and Ballesteros both fell back with disappointing rounds of 76. Faldo would have been much closer to Morgan but for an horrendous eight at the 14th where he hit his ball up into the branches of a large tree where it duly remained (Nick actually

Pebble-dashed: Andy Dillard and Gil Morgan during the third round

Morgan, an eye doctor by profession and redoubtable golfer by trade, was having a whale of a time. In the second round he added an excellent 69 to his first day 66 for a 135 total, increasing his lead in the championship to three strokes. In 36 holes Morgan had scored an incredible fourteen birdies. The only player keeping Morgan within his sights at this stage was Andrew Dillard - much to everyone's amazement. Dillard's commendable 70, which was eleven strokes fewer than 'golden boy' Phil Mickelson could manage, meant that the long distance qualifier would be going out in the final pairing on Saturday. Dillard aside, Morgan held an advantage of at least five shots over the rest of the field. Best of the rest on 140 were Ray Floyd and Australian

contemplated doing a Bernhard Langer after shinning up the trunk like a nine-year-old, but alas couldn't find his ball). Slightly better placed than Faldo and Ballesteros were Masters Champion Fred Couples on 142, Tom Kite and Nick Price on 143 and Ian Woosnam on 144; but even they were between seven and nine shots off the blistering pace set by Morgan. The half way cut fell at 148 meaning that Ballesteros made it by one, but his Ryder Cup partner Olazabal missed out by three. At least José-Maria was in good company for sadly neither Nicklaus nor Watson survived the Pebble Beach axe: how times have changed in ten years!

History was made during the third round of the championship. Morgan went to bed on the Friday evening knowing that he was one birdie away from becoming the first golfer to reach ten under par in a US Open. It took him just three holes on Saturday to pass that magical landmark. More birdies followed and after seven holes he stood at 12 under par: not only had he made history but he was now leading the championship by seven strokes. Dillard struggled from the off, perhaps he was finally coming to terms with his exalted position, and with nobody further down the field making any serious headway it was beginning to look processional; 'Doctor Gil Morgan, US Open champion 1992 - the oldest winner in the history of the event...' Crash! Suddenly in the space of seven holes Morgan's world was turned upside-down. 12 under par after the 7th quickly became three under par after the 14th. A glorious backdrop maybe, but it was not a pretty picture seeing Morgan fumbling and stumbling; it was as if the eye specialist was being treated to a cruel version of blind man's buff. 'Like falling out of the sky wearing a parachute that has a hole in it' was how Morgan later described his ordeal.

To say that Morgan's collapse altered the complexion of the championship would be a gross misstatement: it produced a completely different scenario and gave fresh hope to anyone who had been able to put together a reasonable score on the third day. Morgan of course wasn't completely sunk, and showing admirable courage in adversity, he managed to extract a birdie four from the notorious par five 18th and finished his round on four under par, still leading, albeit now by the smallest of margins. On Friday night only one player had been within five strokes of Morgan, now there were twenty-one, including nine players who had won Major championships. New life had certainly been breathed into the much vaunted European challenge. Of the 66 players who

teed off on Saturday only nine broke 70 but among this group were the 'big three' of Woosnam (69), Faldo (68) and Ballesteros (69): they were now respectively just one, two and four shots off the lead and hopes of a first European success in the championship since Tony Jacklin in 1970 had been rekindled. A little further down the leader board Colin Montgomerie and Anders Forsbrand both carded 77s in the third round (the same as Gil Morgan) and were six shots adrift: Montgomerie let it be known that his goal for the final round was simply to finish in the top 16, this guaranteeing an invitation to the 1993 US Masters. Little did he know what was in store for him on Sunday! In joint second position with Woosnam at the end of the third round were Tom Kite and Mark Brooks. But thanks to the kind Doctor it was almost anybody's championship.

Saturday night's congested leader board contrasted greatly, not just with the state of affairs that had existed 12 hours earlier but also with the situation of 12 months before. The 1991 US Open had developed into a head-to-head type confrontation between Payne Stewart and Scott Simpson long before the end of the third day's play (it of course continued into a fifth day and wasn't settled until Stewart finally clinched victory on the 90th green). Payne Stewart and Scott Simpson - two outstanding golfers; who could possibly have imagined then, or now, that on the Sunday of the 1992 US Open they would shoot 83 and 88 respectively? But then as was outlined earlier this turned into a most extraordinary championship. The reason was straightforward enough: it was the wind. An ill wind for many but a wind that would bring great change to the life of one Thomas Kite Jnr.

The wind was sufficiently strong in the morning to prevent any of the early starters from breaking 70. It increased in intensity around midday, then strengthened yet more early in the afternoon. Beautiful Pebble Beach had turned into the smiler with the knife. 'The toughest conditions I have ever played in' reckoned Colin Montgomerie, a golfer whose swing had been fashioned on windswept Scottish links courses - and he didn't have to confront the cliff top holes at the height of the storm! The leaders did,

a brave par at the last where he managed to get 'up and down' from a greenside bunker, gave him a round of 70 and a level par total of 288 for the championship. When his final putt disappeared into the hole on the 18th green Jack Nicklaus, commentating for American television, exclaimed, 'That's it, it's over'.

And so it seemed, for the leaders, you recall, were being blown into oblivion;

Colin Montgomerie plays for position at the 72nd hole

however, and one by one their hopes were swept into oblivion. Montgomerie, playing at least two hours ahead of the final group reached the turn in a very steady 36, a score good enough in the conditions to move him swiftly through the field: then on the back nine he played a series of outstanding strokes, twice in fact hitting the pin with his approach shots at par four holes. 'Monterey Monty' was making birdies while others were struggling to save pars. Over his closing holes the big Scot began to realise that if he could just keep his feet on terra firma the US Open crown might be his. Although Colin, like countless others, did drop a shot at the 17th,

Morgan was heading for an 81, Woosnam a 79, Brooks an 84, Faldo a 77 and Ballesteros a 79. Even such 'seasoned campaigners' as Ray Floyd and Craig Stadler couldn't cope with the conditions, both taking 81. It was utter carnage. Ah, except for Kite. Tom Kite, 'the best player never to have won a Major' was at last enjoying a slice of good fortune. Despite taking six at the 4th, he was very much in the thick of things when he stood over a 20-foot birdie putt at the 6th. He holed that putt then chipped in for an amazing two at the terrifying short 7th. Slice of good fortune? More like a full loaf. It was an unbelievable stroke in the circumstances,

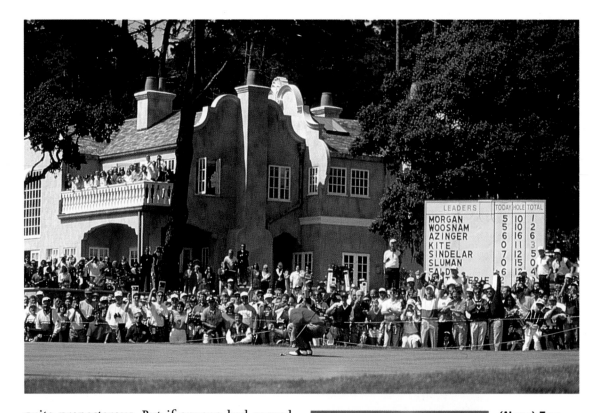

LEADERS	TODAY	HOLE	TOTAL
MORGAN	5	10	1
WOOSNAM	5	10	2
AZINGER	6	16	6
KITE	0	11	3
SINDELAR	7	12	5
SLUMAN	0	15	4
FALD	6	12	

quite preposterous. But if anyone had earned it, it was probably Tom Kite, the biggest 'earner' in the history of golf. Kite survived the next few holes - a genuine case of weathering the storm - and when he turned for home had built himself a sizeable lead, one which with the aid of a tremendous birdie at the 12th he was able to cling on to. Once his drive at the 18th had landed safely on the fairway Kite was able to enjoy the final hole and coast to a two stroke victory. A late flourish from Jeff Sluman relegated Montgomerie to third place, and although he nearly did sneak an amazing victory, if Montgomerie had won the '92 US Open he'd have been known for the rest of his days as 'the Poacher of Pebble Beach'. Who on Sunday morning could possibly have predicted what would happen? No one of course, but with hindsight the cryptic answer was to be found blowing in the wind.

(Above) Tom Kite birdies the 12th in the final round and sets himself up for victory.

'Everything comes to he who waits'. At last Kite wins a Major

1992 US Open

FINAL · SCORES

**Tom Kite,
1992 US Open
Champion**

T Kite	71	72	70	72	285	$275,000
J Sluman	73	74	69	71	287	137,500
C Montgomerie	70	71	77	70	288	84,245
N Faldo	70	76	68	77	291	54,924
N Price	71	72	77	71	291	54,924
I Woosnam	72	72	69	79	292	32,315
J D Blake	70	74	75	73	292	32,315
B Gilder	73	70	75	74	292	32,315
B Andrade	72	74	72	74	292	32,315
M Hulbert	74	73	70	75	292	32,315
T Lehman	69	74	72	77	292	32,315
J Sindelar	74	72	68	78	292	32,315
M McCumber	70	76	73	74	293	22,531
J Cook	72	72	74	75	293	22,531
I Baker-Finch	74	71	72	76	293	22,531
G Morgan	66	69	77	81	293	22,531
T Tyner	74	72	78	70	294	18,069
W Grady	74	66	81	73	294	18,069
F Couples	72	70	78	74	294	18,069
W Wood	70	75	75	74	294	18,069
A Magee	77	69	72	76	294	18,069
A Dillard	68	70	79	77	294	18,069
B Bryant	71	76	75	73	295	13,906
B Mayfair	74	73	75	73	295	13,906
C Strange	67	78	76	74	295	13,906
J Haas	70	77	74	74	295	13,906
J Kane	73	71	76	75	295	13,906
B Langer	73	72	75	75	295	13,906
D Hammond	73	73	73	76	295	13,906
M Ozaki	77	70	72	76	295	13,906
D Hart	76	71	71	77	295	13,906
S Ballesteros	71	76	69	79	295	13,906
F Funk	72	75	76	73	296	10,531
J Delsing	73	73	75	75	296	10,531
C Parry	73	73	73	77	296	10,531
R Cochran	73	74	72	77	296	10,531
A Forsbrand	71	70	77	78	296	10,531
T Purtzer	70	72	76	78	296	10,531
M Calcavecchia	70	73	73	80	296	10,531

R Zokol	72	72	72	80	296	10,531
P Azinger	70	75	71	80	296	10,531
C Stadler	71	72	72	81	296	10,531
M McNulty	74	72	69	81	296	10,531
D Pooley	76	71	76	74	297	8,006
D Pruitt	73	73	74	77	297	8,006
B Estes	72	71	74	80	297	8,006
R Floyd	71	69	76	81	297	8,006
R Mediate	71	75	70	81	297	8,006
G Hallberg	71	70	73	83	297	8,006
M Brooks	70	74	69	84	297	8,006
S Gump	75	72	75	76	298	6,370
S Lyle	73	74	75	76	298	6,370
H Irwin	73	70	78	77	298	6,370
B Wolcott	76	70	74	78	298	6,370
T Schulz	71	75	73	79	298	6,370
P Stewart	73	70	72	83	298	6,370
D Donovan	73	74	76	76	299	5,903
D Waldorf	73	74	76	76	299	5,903
J Gallagher Jr	71	76	69	83	299	5,903
D Love III	72	71	74	83	300	5,773
D Forsman	72	70	74	84	300	5,773
M Smith	74	71	74	82	301	5,773
P Jacobsen	74	71	77	80	302	5,773
G Twiggs	72	71	80	80	302	5,773
S Simpson	76	71	68	88	303	5,773
K Triplett	73	73	80	79	305	5,773

SEVENTH HEAVEN

A Commentary by John Hopkins

• •

I dare say that in those still, quiet moments when Tom Kite is replaying in his mind's eye the events in California in June last year he will remember one stroke above all others. He had 285 in all in the 92nd US Open and goodness knows how many in preparation, but there was one that suggested to him it was going to be his day and not Colin Montgomerie's, Jeff Sluman's or Gil Morgan's.

The stroke came on the 7th hole and it was every bit as significant as the shot Fred Couples had played at the 12th in the US Masters two months earlier. If Kite had made a mess of his he might not be US Open Champion just as had Couples' ball not stopped, somehow, on the bank above Rae's Creek on that last afternoon, it is equally doubtful that he would have won his first Major.

The situation with Kite was as follows. He was five strokes behind Morgan after the first round and eight after 36 holes. Morgan streaked away at the start of the 3rd round and became the first man in the history of the US Open to reach 10 under par. That was not all. Kite was just one of many to be left spread-eagled when Morgan moved, albeit briefly, to 12 under par and into a lead of seven strokes. 'Gil has got the Open in his hands now' said Faldo, who had himself just completed his third round with a 68. 'He is playing great golf and good luck to him. If he blocks everything out and comes back in one or two under, it's his. But if he falls three or four over on the back nine then anything could happen.'

Sure enough, Morgan could not cope with the Open pressure. In the space of seven holes he took three bogeys and three double bogeys and had to sign for a 77, 11 shots worse than his opening round. He retained the lead but it was now down to the narrowest possible margin. Kite, Ian Woosnam and Mark Brooks were just one stroke behind.

The fourth day, Kite's day, was unlike the first three, which had been overcast and calm. Mid-morning the word went around: 'the wind's up'. White horses were dancing on waves out in Carmel Bay and the concluding round at Pebble beach would be played in the sort of conditions one had wanted all week. The full extent of it was emphasised by Colin Montgomerie who started at 10:22. 'When I stood on the 4th tee and looked at the 17th green I thought: 'It's a three or four iron. When I got to the tee myself I realised it had become a three wood or even a driver.'

With the wind freshening all the time Kite played steadily to the 7th and then faced one of golf's most picturesque short holes at its most demanding. It may only be 107 yards long but today, into a wind that was whipping off the sea, it required a five or six iron. Few players could manage the trick of using such a club and keeping the ball on the putting surface. Nick Faldo found himself in a quandary. He remembered what Tom Watson said: 'When the wind blows always take a five iron.' He dithered before selecting a six iron and trying to punch a shot through the wind and succeeded only in hitting it straight left to within a few feet of the top of the cliff, 25 yards from the flag. He escaped with a five.

If this was the hole that cost Faldo the US Open, it was the hole that won it for Kite. When last seen, his tee shot, also hit with a six iron, was heading for the turbulent sea. It stopped where it landed, a few feet from perdition, much as Faldo's had a few moments before.

At this moment Montgomerie was being ushered into a television booth behind the 18th green. The big Scot had shot a marvellous round of 70 to finish on even par 288. Jack Nicklaus welcomed him to the TV studio with the words: 'Congratulations Colin. How does it feel to win your first US Open?'

Nicklaus should have known better. Ten years earlier Jack Whittaker had said something similar to him when he had completed his final round - and then Watson chipped in on the 17th and birdied the 18th to snatch victory. Could lightning strike twice at Pebble Beach? Hardly had the words left Nicklaus' mouth, however, than a great roar went up. Kite had played The Shot. His ball ran across the green, banged into the flag stick and dropped into the hole.

That shot wiped out all the bad memories for Kite: of how he was leading the 1981 US Masters and hit into Rae's Creek in the fourth round; of how he held the lead in the 1985 Open at Sandwich only to take a six on the par four 10th; of how he missed a 12 foot birdie putt on the 72nd green to tie Jack Nicklaus in the 1986 Masters; of how at Oakhill in upstate New York he led after 54 holes of the 1989 US Open, only to run up a seven on the 5th hole of the final round. Kite's chip-in on the 7th did not give him victory but it gave him the platform on which to build. If his ball had missed the flag stick and run off the green a four would have been likely, a five a possibility.

He still had 11 holes to go. At times like these pros say they take one hole at a time. It is a cliché of modern golf but one understands what is meant. It was all Kite could do to concentrate on maintaining his swing and putting stroke without allowing himself to become too concerned about how his rivals were performing.

Suffice to say that Kite coped remarkably well in the conditions. Playing a succession of brave strokes, the new, inspired Tom Kite did not do what kites normally do on windless days and fall to earth. He soared high, he deserved to win his first Major title.

All his life Kite had battled against the odds. He was a small, fat, short-sighted and earnest child with a complexion that was not suited to the prickly heat of Texas where he grew up. By contrast, growing up nearby was a taller, good-looking and gifted golfer named Ben Crenshaw. During their days at the Austin Country Club they would play 18 holes together. Then Crenshaw would dive into the swimming pool while Kite would dive into a bucket of practice balls. 'Ben was glamorous-looking and a long hitter with a picture-book swing,' Kite said. 'I was short off the tee and fat, grinding away, down the middle, on the green and two putts.'

It was a rivalry that matched Sandy Lyle's with Nick Faldo. The success of Crenshaw, who was two years younger, drove Kite on relentlessly, just as Lyle's triumphs made Faldo work even harder. Crenshaw beat Kite to a US Masters but Kite beat Crenshaw to a US Open. 'Dad taught me early that nothing comes to you unless you work hard for it,' Kite recalled. 'He always stressed hard work and self-discipline. He always said to me, 'keep doing your best'.'

That sunny day in California, Kite did his best and it was good enough - thanks, in no small part, to that chip-in.

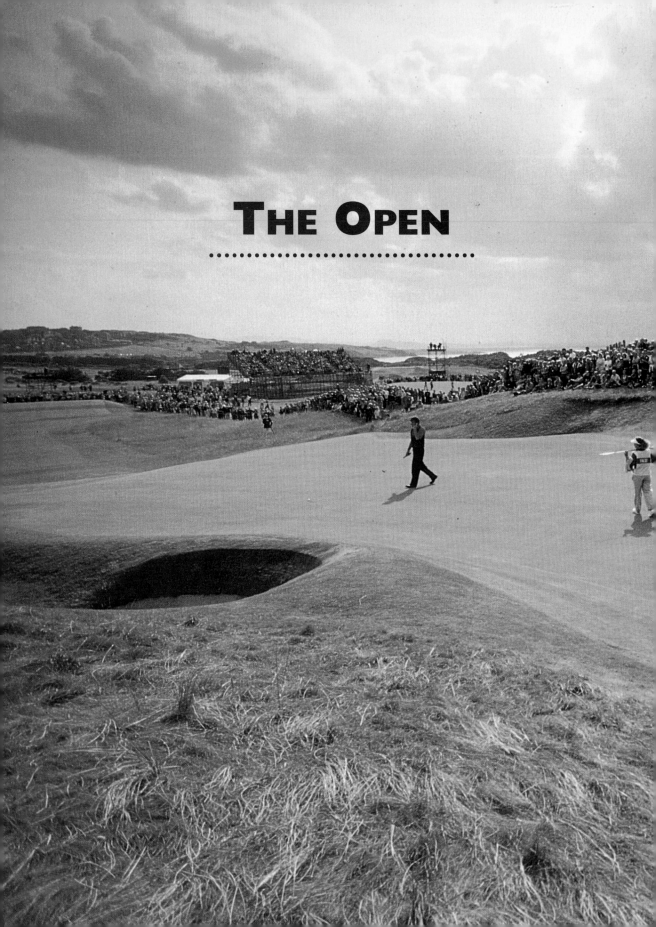

THE OPEN

THE OPEN CHAMPIONSHIP

ROLL · OF · HONOUR

1860	Willie Park	1902	Alexander Herd	1912	Edward Ray
1861	Tom Morris, Sr	1903	Harry Vardon	1913	John H. Taylor
1862	Tom Morris, Sr	1904	Jack White	1914	Harry Vardon
1863	Willie Park	1905	James Braid	1915-19	No championships played
1864	Tom Morris, Sr	1906	James Braid	1920	George Duncan
1865	Andrew Strath	1907	Arnaud Massy	1921	* Jock Hutchison
1866	Willie Park	1908	James Braid	1922	Walter Hagen
1867	Tom Morris, Sr	1909	John H. Taylor	1923	Arthur G. Havers
1868	Tom Morris, Jr	1910	James Braid	1924	Walter Hagen
1869	Tom Morris, Jr	1911	Harry Vardon	1925	James M. Barnes
1870	Tom Morris, Jr				
1871	No championships played				
1872	Tom Morris, Jr				
1873	Tom Kidd				
1874	Mungo Park				
1875	Willie Park				
1876	Bob Martin				
1877	Jamie Anderson				
1878	Jamie Anderson				
1879	Jamie Anderson				
1880	Robert Ferguson				
1881	Robert Ferguson				
1882	Robert Ferguson				
1883	* Willie Fernie				
1884	Jack Simpson				
1885	Bob Martin				
1886	David Brown				
1887	Willie Park, Jr				
1888	Jack Burns				
1889	* Willie Park, Jr				
1890	John Ball				
1891	Hugh Kirkaldy				
1892	Harold H. Hilton				
1893	William Auchterlonie				
1894	John H. Taylor				
1895	John H. Taylor				
1896	* Harry Vardon				
1897	Harold H. Hilton				
1898	Harry Vardon				
1899	Harry Vardon				
1900	John H. Taylor				
1901	James Braid				

1926	Robert T. Jones	1940-45	No championships played	1985	Sandy Lyle
1927	Robert T. Jones	1946	Sam Snead	1986	Greg Norman
1928	Walter Hagen	1947	Fred Daly	1987	Nick Faldo
1929	Walter Hagen	1948	Henry Cotton	1988	Seve Ballesteros
1930	Robert T. Jones	1949	* Bobby Locke	1989	* Mark Calcavecchia
1931	Tommy D. Armour	1950	Bobby Locke	1990	Nick Faldo
1932	Gene Sarazen	1951	Max Faulkner	1991	Ian Baker-Finch
1933	* Denny Shute	1952	Bobby Locke	1992	Nick Faldo
1934	Henry Cotton	1953	Ben Hogan		
1935	Alfred Perry	1954	Peter Thomson		
1936	Alfred Padgham	1955	Peter Thomson	* Winner in play-off.
1937	Henry Cotton	1956	Peter Thomson		
1938	R. A. Whitcombe	1957	Bobby Locke		
1939	Richard Burton	1958	* Peter Thomson		

· HIGHLIGHTS ·

1959	Gary Player	**Most wins:**	
1960	Kel Nagle	6	Harry Vardon
1961	Arnold Palmer	5	Hohn H. Taylor
1962	Arnold Palmer		James Braid
1963	* Bob Charles		Peter Thomson
1964	Tony Lema		Tom Watson

Most times runner-up:

    7 Jack Nicklaus

Biggest margin of victory:

    13 Old Tom Morris (1862)

Lowest winning total:

    268 Tom Watson (1977)

Lowest single round:

    63 Mark Hayes (1977)

       Isao Aoki (1980)

       Greg Norman (1986)

       Paul Broadhurst (1990)

       Jodie Mudd (1991)

Lowest final round by winner:

    65 Tom Watson (1977)

       Severiano Ballesteros (1988)

    64 Greg Norman (tied but lost play-off in 1989)

Oldest champion:

    Old Tom Morris, aged 46 (1867)

Youngest champion:

    Young Tom Morris, aged 17 (1868)

    Severiano Ballesteros (youngest this century, aged 22 in 1979)

1965	Peter Thomson
1966	Jack Nicklaus
1967	Roberto De Vicenzo
1968	Gary Player
1969	Tony Jacklin
1970	* Jack Nicklaus
1971	Lee Trevino
1972	Lee Trevino
1973	Tom Weiskopf
1974	Gary Player
1975	* Tom Watson
1976	Johnny Miller
1977	Tom Watson
1978	Jack Nicklaus
1979	Seve Ballesteros
1980	Tom Watson
1981	Bill Rogers
1982	Tom Watson
1983	Tom Watson
1984	Seve Ballesteros

The Golden Bear, Jack Nicklaus

THE 1992 OPEN

· ·

The 121st Open Championship was all about one man, Nick Faldo; the only player capable of beating him was Nick Faldo ...he gave himself a good run for his money

'If you can kiss the mistress, never kiss the maid'.

There are 365 days in most years - 366 as it happens in 1992 - but only 16 really matter to Nick Faldo. Just as a decade and more ago only 16 really mattered to Jack Nicklaus: the four days of the four Major championships. The fact that Nick Faldo had 'blown' a few tournaments on the European Tour during the run up to the Open Championship at Muirfield last July must have been extremely frustrating for him but it wasn't extremely relevant. The most significant facts were that he arrived superbly prepared and that his form was, in his own words, 'awesome'. Combine these two elements with Faldo's enviable ability to raise his game for the big occasion and you have the recipe for near invincibility. That is why despite the strength and depth of the opposition Nick came to Muirfield as the hottest Open favourite since Nicklaus was in his prime in the mid 1970s.

Faldo was attempting to become the first British golfer since Henry Cotton to win three Open Championships and this was the perfect stage. Muirfield is where Faldo won his first Open title and where Cotton won his last. The key to Cotton's third victory all those years ago (it was 1948 and Britain still had an Empire) was a masterly second round 66, performed with perfect timing - in all

A veteran perhaps, but Ray Floyd scored a 64 on the first day to share the lead

senses of the word - in front of a watching King George VI. Cotton also had the knack of rising to the occasion.

Despite dropping a shot at his very first hole, 66 is the score that Nick Faldo managed (I almost wrote 'chose') to put together on the first day of the 121st Open. It didn't quite give him the early lead in the championship but it immediately planted his name in a prime position on the leader

breeze all day) to compile very impressive rounds of 64 and Britons Ian Woosnam and Gordon Brand Jnr. opened with fine 65s. South Africa's great hope for the future, 22-year-old Ernie Els, matched Faldo's 66, as did 'smiling' John Cook and little known Lee Janzen, a surprise winner on the US Tour in February.

It was early days, but then all four days count, and Nick Faldo was already four

Widely tipped as a future champion, South African Ernie Els made a big impression at Muirfield

board. The sight of the score N. FALDO -5 (18) so early in the championship must have struck fear into the hearts of each and every challenger. Faldo described it as simply, 'a nice looking number'.

Only four players bettered Faldo's 66. The Americans Steve Pate and Ray Floyd both took full advantage of extremely favourable conditions (there was barely more than a soft

strokes ahead of the likes of Seve Ballesteros, Fred Couples, Tom Kite, José-Maria Olazabal and Paul Azinger and five ahead of Australians Greg Norman and the defending champion, Ian Baker-Finch. Nick's eyes were already fixed firmly on the prize. The ultimate prize.

'The higher the plum tree, the riper the plum.'

In a class of
his own:
Nick Faldo at
Muirfield

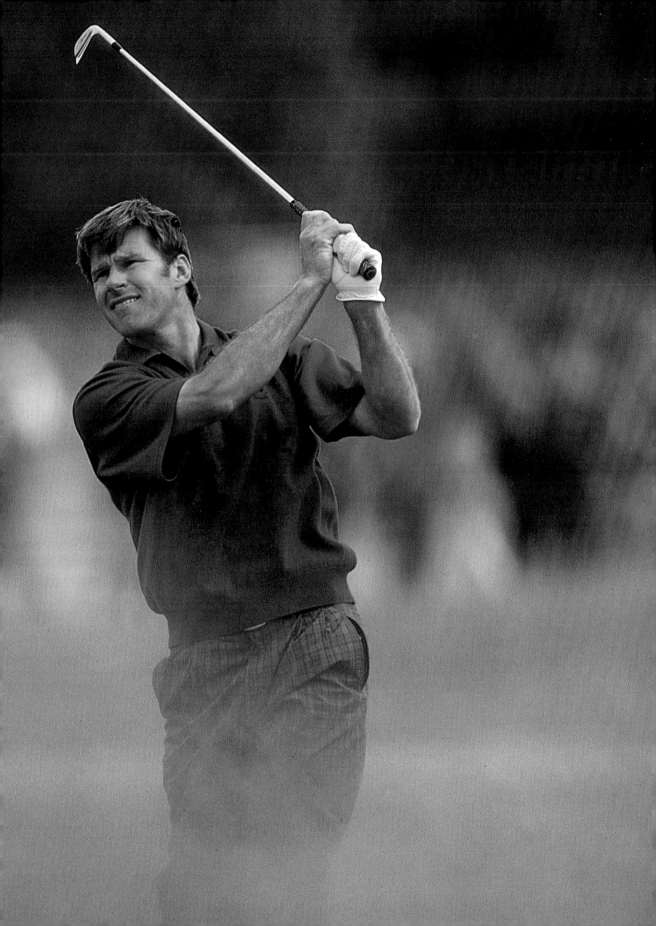

*'If you can't stand the heat,
get out of the kitchen.'*

The second day of the Open was a real Cotton-picking day. It wasn't especially hot, but it was a real sizzler for Nick Faldo who eclipsed the great Henry on two counts and left most of the field out for the count. On Friday Faldo beat Cotton's second round 'command performance' by two strokes with

It was José the Matador on Sunday afternoon, but Olazabal had too much ground to make up

a magnificent 64: 'my best ever round in the Open'. It also bettered by two Henry's 36 hole record for the championship: the total of 132 (67-65) which Cotton achieved in 1934 had been one of the longest standing records in championship golf. 'Fantastic Faldo' roared the newspaper headlines the following morning as they related, almost stroke by stroke, the details of his wonderful round. Those details included a brilliant run of seven 3s in eight holes. (Where now the 'boring par-machine' of 1987?) Where now the rest of the field? In a word, scattered. Only six players lay within seven shots of Faldo's 130 total: Cook and Brand Jnr. were joint second on 133; Pate was on 134 and Floyd, Els and Donnie Hammond were on 135.

Some notable names were suffering a worse fate. Ballesteros walked to the 18th tee of his second round needing a par four to avoid missing the half way cut. He proceeded to play the hole in a way that pretty much summed up his year for he stumbled to a double bogey six, three putting from no distance at all.

As television commentator Bruce Critchley aptly remarked, 'For a proud man that was a horrid way for it to end.' Three former Muirfield champions, Gary Player, Jack Nicklaus and Tom Watson, also failed to make it through to the weekend, as, more surprisingly, did the players occupying first and second positions on the US Tour money list, Masters Champion Fred Couples and The Players Champion Davis Love.

The truth of the matter though was that just about everyone was wilting under the immense pressure exerted by Faldo. He was playing golf on another plane.

*'The same heat that melts the wax
will harden the clay.'*

*'If the mountain will not come to Mahomet,
Mahomet must go to the mountain.'*

The weather at Muirfield on Saturday was dull, and frankly, so was much of the golf. Brilliance, almost by definition, is difficult to sustain and Faldo – at least by his exceptional standards - was forced to settle for a rather workman-like round. Consolidation was the name of the game on Saturday and Faldo did

John Cook nearly stole the show on Sunday – before Faldo rallied and he derailed

it extremely well. But then it was his birthday. On his 35th birthday Nick shot a 69 and he not only consolidated, but actually extended his lead in the championship from three to four. The top of the leader board on Saturday evening looked much as it had done 24 hours earlier: Faldo was now 14 under par with a total of 199 (which equalled his

own 54 hole record set at St Andrews in 1990); Pate and Cook shared second position on 203 and then there was a gap of another two strokes to a group of players on 205, all seemingly jostling for the minor places. The only player ranked among the top 10 in the world within seven shots of the world's number one was Olazabal on 206, but he let it be known that he wasn't harbouring any serious hopes of collecting a first Major title.

As for those players in the field who could boast such a victory, the closest was some nine strokes adrift.

Was it fate, or was it golfing gremlins? Someone, or something determined that the final day's play in the 1992 Open Championship would be anything but dull. In fact it was precisely the opposite: a day of high drama, a day when Nick Faldo experienced just about every emotion it is possible to experience in a Major championship round of golf. It was a day of triumph, tragedy and triumph.

Nick Faldo, Open champion for the third time in six years

There was little warning of what was to come during Faldo's first nine holes. The leader repeated his first round blemish by dropping a stroke at the 1st, but no matter, he soon steadied himself and about two hours later stood over a 10 foot putt for a birdie at the 10th which, if he could hole it, would restore his four stroke cushion.

Up ahead of Faldo two players at last started to make some kind of a challenge. Olazabal birdied the 11th, 12th and 17th to get to 10 under par and Cook, who had earlier run up a seven at the 9th where he drove out of bounds, birdied the 12th, 15th and 16th. Even more significant, and much more staggering, was the fact that Faldo (who missed his birdie putt at the 10th) contrived to bogey the 11th, 13th and 14th.

Was somebody rewriting the script? For three and a half days it had been a one man show, or rather a one man exhibition, but now, incredibly, as Faldo walked to the 15th tee he was two shots behind Cook; 'smiling' John Cook, who was just about to drill a fabulous three iron into the heart of the 17th green to set up a possible eagle three, certain birdie four. It was at this moment that Faldo told himself - and it is a story one suspects he will one day tell his grand children over and over again - that he had better play the best four holes of life. He will want to tell them all because he did precisely that. Of course it helped that Cook did a Scott Hoch when he reached the 17th green and a Paul Azinger when he played the 18th but it is no coincidence that players are apt to perform such acts of generosity when they have Nick Faldo breathing down their neck during the final moments of a Major championship.

Olazabal's 32 on the back nine lifted him into third position ahead of the faltering Pate. Cook's 5-5 finish meant that Faldo, following courageous birdies at the 15th, where he struck a glorious five iron to within three feet of the flag, and the 17th, needed to par the last to win his third Open Championship. And this time he kept to the script.

'Little thieves are hanged, but great ones escape'.

1992 OPEN

FINAL · SCORES

An emotional Faldo raises his arms in triumph

N Faldo	66	64	69	73	272	£95,000
J Cook	66	67	70	70	273	75,000
J M Olazabal	70	67	69	68	274	64,000
S Pate	64	70	69	73	276	53,000
D Hammond	70	65	70	74	279	30,071
A Magee	67	72	70	70	279	30,071
E Els	66	69	70	74	279	30,071
I Woosnam	65	73	70	71	279	30,071
G Brand Jnr	65	68	72	74	279	30,071
M Mackenzie	71	67	70	71	279	30,071
R Karlsson	70	68	70	71	279	30,071
J Spence	71	68	70	71	280	17,383
C Beck	71	68	67	74	280	17,383
R Floyd	64	71	73	72	280	17,383
S Lyle	68	70	70	72	280	17,383
M O'Meara	71	68	72	69	280	17,383
L Rinker	69	68	70	73	280	17,383
G Norman	71	72	70	68	281	13,200
H Irwin	70	73	67	72	282	11,066
I Baker-Finch	71	71	72	68	282	11,066
T Kite	70	69	71	72	282	11,066
P Mitchell	69	71	72	71	283	8,950
P Lawrie	70	72	68	73	283	8,950
T Purtzer	68	69	75	71	283	8,950
B Andrade	69	71	70	74	284	7,700
D Waldorf	69	70	73	72	284	7,700
P Senior	79	69	70	75	284	7,700
M Calcavecchia	69	71	73	72	285	6,658
M McNulty	71	70	70	74	285	6,658
J Mudd	71	69	74	71	285	6,658
C Parry	67	71	76	71	285	6,658
R Cochran	71	68	72	74	285	6,658
M Lanner	72	68	71	74	285	6,658
A Forsbrand	70	72	70	74	286	5,760
C Pavin	69	74	73	70	286	5,760
P Stewart	70	73	71	72	286	5,760
S Elkington	68	70	75	73	286	5,760
T Johnstone	72	71	74	69	286	5,760
D W Basson	71	71	71	74	287	5,083
L Janzen	66	73	73	75	287	5,083
L Trevino	69	71	73	74	287	5,083
S Richardson	74	68	73	72	287	5,083
W Grady	73	69	71	74	287	5,083
R Rafferty	69	71	75	72	287	5,083
M Harwood	72	68	76	72	288	4,675
L Wadkins	69	69	75	75	288	4,675
J Coceres	74	69	73	72	288	4,675
R Mediate	67	75	73	73	288	4,675
C Mann	74	69	72	73	288	4,675
B Marchbank	71	72	71	74	288	4,675
R Mackay	73	70	73	73	289	4,075
V Singh	69	72	76	72	289	4,075
N Price	69	73	73	74	289	4,075
B Lane	73	69	73	74	289	4,075
C Rocca	67	75	73	75	290	3,875
D Feherty	71	70	72	77	290	3,875
M Brooks	71	71	73	75	290	3,875
O Vincent III	67	75	77	71	290	3,875
P Azinger	70	69	75	77	291	3,650
B Langer	70	72	76	73	291	3,650
W Riley	71	72	75	73	291	3,650
W Guy	72	71	70	78	291	3,650
M Clayton	72	70	75	74	291	3,650
C Stadler	72	70	75	75	292	3,425
R Chapman	72	71	71	78	292	3,425
D Mijovic	70	71	80	71	292	3,425
H Buhrmann	70	72	75	75	292	3,425

LIVING FOR THE MOMENT

A Commentary by Derek Lawrenson

• •

It is one of the great ironies of a game that takes years to learn and hours to play that the course of a whole career can be defined in the seconds it takes to complete a single stroke.

Severiano Ballesteros, for example, went from a golfer possessed with consummate self-belief to one riddled with anxiety in the moment it took for a poorly struck four iron to the 15th at Augusta in 1986 to finish in the water that fronts the green.

Similarly, Tom Watson has never erased the haunting memory of a two iron to the 17th at St Andrews in 1984 that finished over the green and on what has proved a road to oblivion.

The place in history of these two great exponents of the Royal and Ancient art is, of course, assured but how much more would they have won had these shots not occurred just when they were in their prime?

A superficial observer of the situation might wonder how so much achievement can be undermined by so small a mistake, but it is precisely these strokes that determine a golfer's place in the grand scheme of things.

It is on the ability to hit greens in the final holes of a Major championship that a great player earns such status, why he makes such great sacrifices and when it all unravels, the disappointment can be crushing.

Nick Faldo unravelled his swing all those years ago and pieced it back together again purely on flimsy, but for him overwhelming evidence, that it could not withstand the innate pressures induced by being in contention to win a Major.

He had no desire to be 20th in the world. He wanted to be number one. And the result of three years' penance was to be able to stand in the middle of the 18th fairway at Muirfield in 1987 and hit a five iron just exactly as he wanted to win the Open.

Five years on Faldo returned to the course of the Honourable Company of Edinburgh Golfers as an overwhelming favourite, a litany of achievement having been assembled in the intervening years.

Yet behind the aura of confidence that surrounded his challenge there lingered the smallest vestiges of doubt. Such was Faldo's form he had been in contention in practically every event leading up to the Open. Yet in the final rounds there had been uncharacteristic collapses.

But all this nagged merely at the back of the mind, compared to the fact that Faldo, Britain's other Mr Major, was back at his beloved Muirfield. And sure enough, after three rounds, Faldo was four shots ahead...

The bookmakers stopped taking bets. The newspapers crowned him Open champion. The final round looked merely a lap of honour, as indeed it had been two years earlier, over the oldest of Old Courses.

But the indication that this was to be rather a different finale was there from the off. The doubts began on Faldo's opening drive which flew unerringly into the one spot on the 1st it was imperative to avoid. Finish in the fairway bunker and a bogey follows as surely as night follows day. This was going to be no final round of 18 straight pars. And for the next three hours Faldo endured a level of mental torture we cannot begin to comprehend. We are used to seeing a marathon runner tottering over the finishing line, his physical energies totally drained. But in the whole history of sport have we witnessed before a man in just such a state owing to mental stress?

The final outcome was as important to Faldo's future as those shots had been in earlier times to Ballesteros and Watson. When the American John Cook stood over an 18 inch putt on the penultimate hole for a two stroke lead and almost certain victory it is no exaggeration to say he had in his hands Faldo's career. For how could Faldo, a man who lives for the Major championships, have possibly coped with the realisation that he had blown a four shot lead in the most important one of all?

Just as Ballesteros' 'destino', his belief that he was destined to become the greatest player of all time, was shattered by that 'fat' four iron that cost him the Masters, so all that Faldo and his coach David Leadbetter had strived for was now on the line. For by this stage the tournament had gone beyond mere disappointment or triumph but had developed epic proportions and become the pivotal moment in Faldo's professional life.

Even in the immediate aftermath of this greatest triumph, Faldo appreciated the enormity of what had been at stake: 'If I had lost I shudder to think what would have happened to me. It would have needed a very big plaster to have covered that one up. Maybe I wouldn't have bothered trying. Maybe I'd have become a fishing professional.'

Cook missed, as we know, and a bogey at the final hole placed Faldo's fate firmly back in his own hands.

Now the pendulum swung. When Faldo completed the shots that were necessary over the 17th and 18th holes, he gained still more

self-belief. The plaudits rang out. Michael Bonallack, the secretary of the Royal and Ancient, saluted him as the best British player of all time. The rest of the year turned out to be about one man as Faldo carried all before him.

He has now become the undisputed Lord of the Links. To date, he has compiled no fewer than 24 rounds in the 60s in the Open, and a true measure of this level of achievement is that he is in sight of Nicklaus' record of 31 in this department, even though he has played in barely half the number of the great man's championships.

The statistics become self-perpetuating. Faldo adds to them because they stand there as reminders of what he has done and can do again. But at Muirfield, we saw how fine the line really is between success and failure.

The Open encapsulated the glory of the game, its great uncertainty, and how a man who one day is king of all he surveys can be humbled the next. Cook's missed 18 inch putt allowed Faldo to breathe once more and escape the suffocating experience that so choked Watson and Ballesteros.

And so on he goes, his triumphs now so great as to make Bonallack's words of praise really not much than a paean of the obvious.

It took his Major championship tally to five out of the last 21 played, a strike rate that were it to continue for the rest of his prime years would certainly take him alongside Watson and Gary Player as the most decorated of players in the modern era, the incomparable Nicklaus excepted.

But while others made these predictions for him and talked about the future, Faldo was content and remains content to sit gratefully in the present. The final round at Muirfield taught him the ultimate lesson. That in Major championship golf you never live for anything other than the moment.

THE USPGA

THE USPGA

ROLL · OF · HONOUR

1916	James M. Barnes
1917-18	No championships played
1919	James M. Barnes
1920	Jock Hutchison
1921	Walter Hagen
1922	Gene Sarazen
1923	Gene Sarazen
1924	Walter Hagen
1925	Walter Hagen
1926	Walter Hagen
1927	Walter Hagen
1928	Leo Diegel
1929	Leo Diegel
1930	Tommy Armour
1931	Tom Creavy
1932	Olin Dutra
1933	Gene Sarazen
1934	Paul Runyan
1935	Johnny Revolta
1936	Denny Shute
1937	Denny Shute
1938	Paul Runyan
1939	Henry Picard
1940	Byron Nelson
1941	Vic Ghezzi
1942	Sam Snead
1943	No championship played
1944	Bob Hamilton
1945	Byron Nelson
1946	Ben Hogan
1947	Jim Ferrier
1948	Ben Hogan
1949	Sam Snead
1950	Chandler Harper
1951	Sam Snead
1952	Jim Turnesa
1953	Walter Burkemo
1954	Chick Harbert
1955	Doug Ford
1956	Jack Burke
1957	Lionel Hebert

Tom Watson still needs a win in the USPGA to complete his Grand Slam set

1958	Dow Finsterwald
1959	Bob Rosburg
1960	Jay Hebert
1961	* Jerry Barber
1962	Gary Player
1963	Jack Nicklaus
1964	Bobby Nichols
1965	Dave Marr
1966	Al Geiberger
1967	* Don January
1968	Julius Boros
1969	Ray Floyd
1970	Dave Stockton
1971	Jack Nicklaus
1972	Gary Player
1973	Jack Nicklaus
1974	Lee Trevino
1975	Jack Nicklaus
1976	Dave Stockton
1977	* Lanny Wadkins

1978	* John Mahaffey
1979	* David Graham
1980	Jack Nicklaus
1981	Larry Nelson
1982	Ray Floyd
1983	Hal Sutton
1984	Lee Trevino
1985	Hubert Green
1986	Bob Tway
1987	* Larry Nelson
1988	Jeff Sluman
1989	Payne Stewart
1990	Wayne Grady
1991	John Daly
1992	Nick Price

* Winner in play-off.

· HIGHLIGHTS ·

Most wins:
  5 Walter Hagen
     Jack Nicklaus
Most times runner-up:
  4 Jack Nicklaus
Biggest margin of victory:
  7 Jack Nicklaus (1980)
Lowest winning total:
  271 Bobby Nichols (1964)
Lowest single round:
  63 Bruce Crampton (1975)
       Ray Floyd (1982)
       Gary Player (1984)
Lowest final round by winner:
  65 David Graham (1979)
       Jeff Sluman (1988)
Oldest champion:
       Julius Boros, aged 48 (1968)
Youngest champion:
       Gene Sarazen, aged 20 (1922)

THE 1992 USPGA

· ·

**We all thought that a non-American golfer
called Nick would triumph at Bellerive...
and how right we were!**

Hot August days and the fourth and final Major of the year had arrived. Between them Arnold Palmer, Tom Watson, Seve Ballesteros and Nick Faldo have won no fewer than twenty-five Major championships, yet strangely not one of them has ever won a USPGA title. It is safe to say that Palmer never will and that time is running out quickly for Watson – which is a great pity, for he needs a win in this championship to become only the fifth player in history to have won all four of golf's Grand Slam events, the feat having been achieved only by Gene Sarazen, Ben Hogan, Gary Player and Jack Nicklaus. Ballesteros has never really threatened to win the USPGA, and given the nature of the courses that are traditionally selected to stage the championship, there is probably only a slight chance that he ever will. Certainly Ballesteros gave himself no hope whatsoever last year when he declined to enter - a combination it seems of bad form, a bad back and perhaps a touch of babyitus as well (son number two was due to enter the world within a few weeks of the anticipated 'sauna in St Louis').

And what about Nick Faldo? The odds on his one day winning golf's fourth Major must be a good deal shorter than those that might be offered on Ballesteros. For one thing his game and temperament would appear much more suited to taming the ultra-demanding, near sadistically prepared PGA type lay-outs; patient, indomitable golfers, not swashbucklers normally win this championship. (But what if it were a match play event, as indeed it once was, you ask... but that's another story!) If Faldo does fail to win the USPGA he may, in years to come, look back at 1992 as the year when he really should have succeeded.

The 74th USPGA Championship was played at the Bellerive Country Club, on the outskirts of St Louis, Missouri. It was here, in 1965 that Gary Player won his one and only US Open title. The Robert Trent Jones-designed course is widely regarded as one of the toughest in America, 'much more difficult than Pebble Beach and compared with it, Augusta is a piece of cake,' according to Colin Montgomerie. The Scotsman was one of 31 overseas players who had either qualified or been invited to wrestle the championship from John Daly (not that anyone, I imagine, would seriously want to wrestle with John Daly).

Aside from Faldo, who in his own words, had 'never been playing better' and whose determination to do well was plain for all to see, several of the 'big guns' were either out of form or out of practice. Ballesteros, as already mentioned, was conspicuous by his absence while Masters Champion Couples and the man he succeeded as champion, Ian Woosnam, had not hit a ball in anger since the Open at Muirfield.

A frequently employed excuse for performing poorly in the USPGA is the weather: too hot and too humid, in a nutshell. August is rarely a pleasant month for playing championship golf in the mid or southern states of America. Soon after winning the Open Faldo was asked how he

was joined by the little known Gene Sauers, from Savannah, Georgia. Three players managed 68: Brian Claar, Jay Don Blake and Nick Faldo. So the Open Champion had made an encouraging start – even if, as he admitted, he'd been a trifle fortunate to hole so many important par-saving putts. Nick had played in the company of the year's two other Major winners, Fred Couples, who had an adventurous 69 and Tom Kite, who took

Gene Sauers led the championship for three days

intended preparing for Bellerive, 'I am going to have to practice in a bathroom with all the taps on,' he said. As it turned out Bellerive wasn't nearly as hot or humid as many had feared.

Basking at the top of the leader board after the first day's play was the 'Walrus', Craig Stadler, who scored a fine 67, and he

73. Apart from Faldo only three other overseas players bettered the par of 71, namely New Zealander Frank Nobilo, with a splendid 69, and Vijay Singh and Nick Price, who both returned steady rounds of 70. Fifteen American players scored 70 or better.

The following evening Sauers, our journeyman from Georgia, was still perched at the top of the leader board. He had added a 69 to his first round 67 for a most impressive 136 total. Behind him the field was starting to string out. Jim Gallagher Jnr., who finished third to John Daly in 1991, left-hander Russ Cochran and Nick Faldo (despite a 5-5 finish) were his closest pursuers on 138 and only Craig Stadler and England's Steven Richardson, courtesy of a marvellous 66, were the right side of the 140 mark. As for the so called 'big guns', Kite, Norman, Azinger, Stewart, Langer and Pavin were all drifting somewhere between 144 and 146. Defending champion Daly and the highly rated Davis Love only narrowly avoided missing the half way cut on 148, which is more than can be said of Olazabal, Woosnam and Lyle. About what price Nick

Faldo now? Or perhaps that should read, now what about Nick Price, Faldo?

The popular Zimbabwean, remember, had opened with a 'steady 70' now after 36 holes he was handily placed on 140. Earlier in the year Price had finished joint fourth in the US Open (level with Faldo) and joint sixth in the US Masters (one stroke ahead of Faldo); few people had been tipping him as a likely winner at Bellerive but as in the case of Ian Baker-Finch before the 1991 Open at Birkdale he was widely regarded as something of a dark horse, someone certainly capable of winning a Major - as his near misses at Royal Troon (1982) and Royal Lytham (1988) clearly demonstrated - but not an obvious choice. There was, however, an omen. The man carrying Nick Price's bag

Newly-crowned Open champion Nick Faldo explodes at Bellerive

at Bellerive was the same caddie who had guided John Daly to his remarkable triumph at Crooked Stick. Jeff 'Squeaky' Medlen is Nick Price's regular caddie and it was only because Price withdrew from the 1991 USPGA at the eleventh hour (an even more urgent case of babyitus) that Medlen ever teamed up with super-sub Daly.

Back to Sauers. Could he keep it going? If he could it wouldn't be so much Gene the

successive birdies from the 9th, was making his move (he finished with a 68), two other players were making the headlines. Bursting out of the pack of 'also-rans', came Jeff Maggert. Jeff who? 'I'm just an average, run of the mill, boring guy' explained the 28-year-old Texan. So average and boring that he was able to shoot 31 on the back nine for a course record 65. Modesty Maggert now joined Price at five under par in second

Nick Price drives during the final round. Jeff Maggert (right) on his way to a course record 65 on Saturday

journeyman as Gene the genie. His riposte to all those who predicted he would crumble at the start of the weekend was to advance from six under par to seven under par with a rock solid round of 70, the highlight of which was a stunning eagle three at the 17th.

While Sauers was quietly and confidently going about his business, and Price, with four

place, two behind Sauers. The other person making news - for all the wrong reasons - was Nick Faldo. After opening with five straight pars, his putting touch suddenly deserted him. Six bogeys later the Open Champion was signing for a 76. It was inexplicable. And it cost him the championship. Now eight shots behind

Sauers and six behind Maggert and Price, Faldo's hopes of a first PGA title had been effectively dashed. On the final day he would rally superbly but the damage had already been done.

The two golfers best placed to challenge the leading trio after the third round were Joe Gallagher Jnr. and John Cook who were four behind Sauers' on 210, three under par. Cook had enjoyed the second best round on Saturday, a very fine 67, which at least gave him an outside chance of capturing a first Grand Slam title just three weeks after coming so agonisingly close at Muirfield.

A hot August day and the fourth day of the fourth Major had arrived.

Poor Sauers and poor Maggert, they were about to become the fall guys. They were about to discover that scoring course record 65s and rock solid 70s on the Saturday of a Major championship is one thing but reproducing the same form on Sunday is another matter.

Sauers was the first to crack. After four holes he had progressed his score to eight under par, but by the time he walked off the 12th green he had dropped all the way back to three under par. Maggert meanwhile was playing some of the best boring, run of the mill golf ever seen at Bellerive. After his 65 on Saturday he played the first nine on Sunday in 34, at which point he led the championship by two from Nick 'nine straight pars' Price. As he turned for home Maggert must have started to think of a victory speech but between the 12th and the 17th he did a Sauers, dropping five shots in six holes. Between them, Sauers and Maggert

The pressures of leading a Major championship finally caught up with Sauers and Maggert

had opened the door for Price and this time no one was waiting to slam it back in his face. Cook and Gallagher could never quite get close enough and though Price's heart must have missed a few beats when he threatened to make a hash of the par five 17th his putter saved the day from 14 feet. Like Couples at Augusta, Kite at Pebble Beach and Faldo at Muirfield, Price parred the final hole for a hugely popular victory. Cook, Sauers, Gallagher Jnr. and the fast-finishing Faldo (his superb 67 - four birdies and fourteen pars - was the best score of the day) all shared second place, one stroke ahead of Maggert, but three behind Price.

The first ever Zimbabwean winner of a Major championship had richly deserved his success and he had learned how to win the hard way. 'If you keep playing as you played today then one day you will be a champion,' Ballesteros told him after their epic duel at Lytham. Put another way, sometimes to win a Major you first have to lose one or two. Come in John Cook, are you reading me?

The putt that saved the blushes – Price at the 17th. (Left) only the caddie had been there before: the moment of victory

1992 USPGA

FINAL · SCORES

Nick Price and the famous Wannamaker trophy

N Price	70	70	68	70	278	$280,000							
N Faldo	68	70	76	67	281	101,250							
J Gallagher Jr	72	66	72	71	281	101,250							
J Cook	71	72	67	71	281	101,250							
G Sauers	67	69	70	75	281	101,250							
J Maggert	71	72	65	74	282	60,000							
R Cochran	69	69	76	69	283	52,500							
D Forsman	70	73	70	70	283	52,500							
D Waldorf	74	73	68	69	284	40,000							
A Forsbrand	73	71	70	70	284	40,000							
B Claar	68	73	73	70	284	40,000							
J Sluman	73	71	72	69	285	30,166							
C Pavin	71	73	70	71	285	30,166							
B Andrade	72	71	70	72	285	30,166							
B Faxon	72	69	75	70	286	24,000	D Edwards	74	70	77	70	291	5,162
G Norman	71	74	71	70	286	24,000	M James	75	72	72	72	291	5,162
M Brooks	71	72	68	75	286	24,000	B R Brown	72	75	72	72	291	5,162
J Huston	73	75	71	68	287	19,000	L Mize	74	74	71	72	291	5,162
R Fehr	74	73	71	69	287	19,000	F Allem	74	72	72	73	291	5,162
S Elkington	74	70	71	72	287	19,000	B Langer	72	74	72	73	291	5,162
T Purtzer	72	72	74	70	288	14,000	L Wadkins	72	71	73	75	291	5,162
L Janzen	74	71	72	71	288	14,000	R Mediate	72	68	74	77	291	5,162
B Britton	70	77	70	71	288	14,000	P Senior	71	76	73	72	292	3,687
F Couples	69	73	73	73	288	14,000	B Bryant	75	71	73	73	292	3,687
T Kite	73	73	69	73	288	14,000	S Pate	70	78	70	74	292	3,687
T Nakajima	71	75	69	73	288	14,000	M Calcavecchia	74	69	74	75	292	3,687
G Morgan	71	69	73	75	288	14,000	V Singh	70	73	73	76	292	3,687
N Ozaki	76	72	74	67	289	9,000	C Stadler	67	72	75	78	292	3,687
M Hulbert	74	74	70	71	289	9,000	S Richardson	73	66	75	78	292	3,687
T Wargo	72	72	73	72	289	9,000	R Floyd	69	75	69	79	292	3,687
P Jacobsen	73	71	72	73	289	9,000	J Sindelar	72	75	75	71	293	3,000
L Nelson	72	68	75	74	289	9,000	L Rinker	72	75	73	73	293	3,000
B Fabel	72	76	74	68	290	7,000	K Clearwater	73	72	74	74	293	3,000
D Love III	77	71	70	72	290	7,000	B Tway	74	73	72	74	293	3,000
B Fleisher	70	72	75	73	290	7,000	G Hallberg	71	72	72	78	293	3,000
F Nobilo	69	74	74	73	290	7,000	J Overton	73	73	76	72	294	2,725
C Montgomerie	72	76	69	73	290	7,000	B McCallister	73	75	76	70	294	2,725
D Pruitt	73	70	73	74	290	7,000	J Haas	75	73	74	72	294	2,725
P Azinger	72	73	68	77	290	7,000	T Watson	72	71	73	78	294	2,725

EXPERIENCE AND THE ART OF WINNING

A Commentary by David Davies

· ·

It is, as we all know, a cruel old world, one that is full of failures. You win a few, but you lose a great many more, and nowhere is this better exemplified than in professional golf. The most successful player the game have ever known, Jack Nicklaus, has, for instance, won the amazing number of 18 Majors, a figure that will probably never be equalled. But in order to be able to do that, he has so far played in 128 championships, which means, of course, that he has 'failed' on 110 occasions. Worse, although he has won on 94 occasions world-wide, he has played in approximately 610 events in order to do so, and while that is a magnificent strike rate in golfing terms, it does mean 516 'failures'.

Golf, given the transitory nature of form within the sport, is one of the hardest at which to be consistently successful and it is also one of the hardest at which to reach one of its four peaks, the Major championships. The history of the game is littered with the names of truly wonderful practitioners of the sport who have narrowly avoided history by failing to win a championship. Until Sunday August 16th 1992 it rather looked as if Nick Price, nice guy and exceedingly good golfer, was going to be of their company. Everyone knew that he was sufficiently talented to win a Major, but everyone also knew that on the two occasions he had been given a real chance at such a title, he had failed.

But on that Sunday, at the Bellerive Country Club in St Louis, Nick Price got the reward he had striven for in 15 years of professional golf; his first Major, the 74th US PGA Championship.

There was general rejoicing at the fact of his win. Not only is Price a thoroughly pleasant man but he had been widely recognised as one of the top three or four players who were the best in the world never to have won a Major. He did it in convincing fashion, too, winning by three shots from a clutch of players who included the world's number one, Nick Faldo. Price's win laid to rest all the conjecture as to whether he was really fitted for a life at the very top of the professional tree. He was two behind Gene Sauers going into the last round and level with Jeff Maggert, a talented but so far unknown player. Of all the people on the leader-board, Price had the most experience, but as far as Majors went, it was experience of the wrong kind. Twice he led the Open Championship in the last round, twice he should have won and twice, of course, he had not. Memories like that can scar a man, or they can, given that the sufferer has the right character, inspire him. Price chose the latter route, surging past Sauers early in the piece and then, by dint of holing two vital putts later on, resisting all advances.

It had been different ten years earlier, in 1982 at Troon. Price was then 25, and whilst he was obviously a good player, he had a quick walk and a quickish temper.

He was also inexperienced, for he had won only two tournaments that had any kind of cachet, the Swiss Open and the South African Masters. When it came to the last round of the Open he lay 86th in the year's European Order of Merit, and there was nothing much in the confidence bank on which he could draw.

Nevertheless he went to the turn in 36 and then started back with three straight birdies. Although his chief challenger, Tom Watson, had earlier eagled the long 11th, Price put that out of his head - for a while. Playing almost an hour behind the American, who only weeks before had won the US Open with that incredible chip-in at the 17th at Pebble Beach, Price was in the unenviable position of knowing exactly what was required of him. Eventually it came down to the fact that if he could play the last five holes in level par, or even one over, he would win the Open. Even two over par would get him in to a play-off.

But he was not even equal to that. The hugely difficult 15th cost him a double-bogey six after he had put his second into a bunker and the 17th, where he was short of the green, cost him a bogey four.

It was the old, old story of the occasion being too much for talented inexperience, a fact that was recognised by Watson, the winner. 'I had it given to me,' he said.

The following year, Price went to play the American Tour and, in the autumn, signalled his presence by winning the World Series, an event that is valuable not just for a huge first prize but for the fact that it offers a 10-year exemption from qualifying for the Tour. Price, it seemed, was set.

But as the years went by, so his reputation for not being quite of championship material grew. He was not to win another US Tour event until 1991 and in the interim, in 1988, he 'lost' another Major. This time though, the manner of his defeat was such that no blame could be attached to his performance. If a man's gotta do what a man's gotta do, then Price did it - only to be totally outgunned by Seve Ballesteros, or as he said,

'One of the best players in the world having one of his best days.'

But that learning experience was, literally, priceless. He learned that there is nothing you can do about what is going on around you: all you can do is play your best golf and hope that it is sufficient.

So when the time came, at Bellerive 1992, to discard the 'best to have never' title, he had some valuable thoughts to draw upon. 'I've had so many tournaments,' he said, 'when I've hit the ball flawlessly from the tee to green, but then holed nothing, that I felt that this time, if I just kept my patience, I would do well. Major championships are usually won by the guy who doesn't make mistakes and I was trying not to make any bogeys. So many times in the past it's been me who's made the mistakes, but I had a good feeling in the final round.'

That feeling fed off a stroke he played at the long 8th, a hole where the field, in general, laid up with their second shot. Price went for it, with a one iron shot that felt so good that even while it was in flight player turned to caddie and said: 'I'm ready.'

It was a stroke that turned a nearly man into a full-blooded achiever. It told him that, despite the pressures, despite the previous failures, this day, this week, he was playing well enough to win. There were still plenty of strokes to be played, of course, but they were played with an inner confidence that gave him the necessary strength.

So now, at last, Price has won a Major championship, the thing that sets players apart when, at the end, their careers are assessed. He is still only 35 and has no doubts as to what he wants to achieve now that he has broken through the invisible barrier.

'I really want to win three or four more,' he says, 'and all of them at least once.'

3

THE WORLD CUP

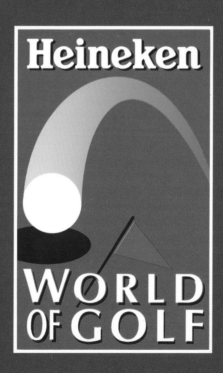

THE WORLD CUP

ROLL · OF · HONOUR

1953	Argentina	Roberto de Vicenzo	Antonio Cerda	Beaconsfield GC, Montreal, Canada
1954	Australia	Peter Thomson	Kel Nagle	Laval-sur-le-Lac GC, Montreal, Canada
1955	United States	Ed Furgol	Chick Harbert	Columbia GC, Washington DC, USA
1956	United States	Ben Hogan	Sam Snead	Wentworth Club, Surrey, England
1957	Japan	T Nakamura	Koichi Ono	Kasumigaseki CC, Tokyo, Japan
1958	Ireland	Harry Bradshaw	Christy O'Connor	Club de Golf Mexico, Mexico
1959	Australia	Peter Thomson	Kel Nagle	Royal Melbourne GC, Melbourne, Australia
1960	United States	Arnold Palmer	Sam Snead	Portmarnock GC, Dublin, Ireland
1961	United States	Sam Snead	Jimmy Demaret	Dorado Beach GC, Dorado Beach, Puerto Rico
1962	United States	Arnold Palmer	Sam Snead	Jockey Club Golf, Buenos Aires, Argentina
1963	United States	Jack Nicklaus	Arnold Palmer	Golf de St-Nom-la-Breteche, Paris, France
1964	United States	Jack Nicklaus	Arnold Palmer	Royal Kaanapali GC, Maui, Hawaii
1965	South Africa	Gary Player	Harold Henning	RACE del Club de Campo, Madrid, Spain
1966	United States	Jack Nicklaus	Arnold Palmer	Tokyo Yomiuri CC, Tokyo, Japan
1967	United States	Jack Nicklaus	Arnold Palmer	Club de Golf Mexico, Mexico City, Mexico
1968	Canada	Al Balding	George Knudson	Circolo Golf Olgiata, Rome, Italy
1969	United States	Lee Trevino	Orville Moody	Singapore Island CC, Singapore
1970	Australia	David Graham	Bruce Devlin	Jockey Club Golf, Buenos Aires, Argentina
1971	United States	Jack Nicklaus	Lee Trevino	PGA National GC, Palm Beach, Florida, USA
1972	Republic of China	Hsieh Min-Nan	Lu Liang-Huan	Royal Melbourne GC, Melbourne, Australia
1973	United States	Johnny Miller	Jack Nicklaus	Golf Nueva Andalucia, Marbella, Spain
1974	South Africa	Bobby Cole	Dale Hayes	Lagunita CC, Caracas, Venezuela
1975	United States	Johnny Miller	Lou Graham	Navatanee GC, Bangkok, Thailand
1976	Spain	Manuel Pinero	Seve Ballesteros	Mission Hills CC, Rancho Mirage, California, USA
1977	Spain	Antonio Garrido	Seve Ballesteros	Wack Wack G & CC, Manila, Philippines
1978	United States	John Mahaffey	Andy North	Princeville Makai GC, Kauai, Hawaii
1979	United States	John Mahaffey	Hale Irwin	Glyfada GC, Athens, Greece
1980	Canada	Dan Halldorson	Jim Nelford	El Rincon Club, Bogota, Columbia
1981	No Tournament			
1982	Spain	Manuel Pinero	José-Maria Canizares	Pierre Marques GC, Acapulco, Mexico
1983	United States	Rex Caldwell	John Cook	Pondok Indah GC, Jakarta, Indonesia
1984	Spain	Jose-Maria Canizares	Jose Rivero	Olgiata GC, Rome, Italy
1985	Canada	Dave Barr	Dan Halldorson	La Quinta GC, California, USA
1986	No Tournament			
1987	Wales	Ian Woosnam	David Llewellyn	Kapalua Bay GC, Maui, Hawaii
1988	United States	Ben Crenshaw	Mark McCumber	Royal Melbourne GC, Melbourne, Australia
1989	Australia	Peter Fowler	Wayne Grady	Club de Golf Las Brisas, Marbella, Spain
1990	Germany	Bernhard Langer	Torsten Giedeon	Grand Cypress Resort, Florida, USA
1991	Sweden	Per-Ulrik Johansson	Anders Forsbrand	La Querce GC, Rome, Italy
1992	United States	Fred Couples	Davis Love	La Moraleja, Madrid, Spain

International Trophy (Leading Individual) Winners
3 wins: Jack Nicklaus, 1963, 1964, 1971
2 wins: Roberto de Vicenzo (1962, 1970); Stan Leonard (1954, 1959);
Johnny Miller (1973, 1975); Gary Player (1965, 1977); Ian Woosnam (1987, 1991)

THE 1992 WORLD CUP OF GOLF

La Moraleja II, Madrid, Spain, November 5-8

Veni, vidi, vici: an early November's day and a dusky Spanish dusk. The new course at La Moraleja, on the golfing fringes of Madrid had been basking in glorious autumnal sunshine for four days and now the American 'dream team' was basking in a reflected glory of its own. Fred Couples and Davis Love had come, seen and conquered - and were about to jet off into the sunset with a chest full of Spanish gold.

But it could have been - and very nearly was - oh so different.

(Above): the magnificent World Cup trophy; from 1993 the event is to be sponsored by Heineken. (Right) the dust (and dusk) settles over La Moraleja

The 1992 World Cup will be long remembered for it produced one of the most exciting and dramatic finishes in the history of international team golf. If Couples and Love were always destined to play starring roles in that drama the Swedish pair of Anders Forsbrand and Per-Ulrik Johansson so excelled in their supporting roles that just before the curtains fell they nearly stole the show - never mind the Spanish gold! There were others, too, who helped make it such a memorable occasion; notably Ian Woosnam of Wales and Brett Ogle of Australia who jousted all week long for the International Trophy, awarded to the leading individual performer. Like the team prize it was only decided by a winning birdie putt on the final green (which in the case of the individual

prize was in fact a sudden death hole).

Although Sweden were the defending champions - the same duo having won for their country a first ever World Cup in Rome the previous November (a more appropriate case then, come to think of it, of veni, vidi, vici) - the Americans were clear favourites to win at La Moraleja. Just a few days earlier Couples and Love had concluded their American seasons finishing in first and

The Old World and The New: host nation Spain were paired with the United States on Saturday (right). (Below left) Wales' captain Ian Woosnam ponders what might have been; (below right) Fred Couples and his famous, lazy swing

second places respectively on the US Tour Money List; both had won three tournaments and more than a million dollars; Couples had won The Masters and Love the Players Championship. Enough said. And they started like hot favourites with Couples scoring a first round 66 and Love a 68 for an immediate two stroke advantage over host nation Spain. Their lead increased after the second day's play to three but was cut back to one after all the teams had completed 54 holes.

That Saturday night leader board was extremely congested. The Americans had a total of 413; Sweden (eight shots behind after the first day) were on 414 and three teams, Spain, Wales and Germany were on 416, a stroke ahead of Australia – six teams separated by just four strokes.

On the final day, Spain (though, without wanting to be unkind, in Rivero and Jimenez they were only fielding a '2nd XI' side) couldn't pull off a famous victory in front of an enthusiastic home crowd and there was one big reason why neither Wales, Germany nor Australia could quite get close enough to challenge the two leading teams: they were too reliant on the performance of one team member only. Woosnam, Langer and Ogle played superbly throughout the week (Ogle eventually defeating Woosnam in the above mentioned individual prize play-off) but unfortunately their playing partners couldn't find their best form. By contrast, both Americans and Swedes were playing first class golf.

For nine holes the two leading teams matched each other stroke for stroke with

The eagle has landed! Sweden's Per-Ulrik Johannson is ecstatic after holing a 40-footer for an eagle three on the 16th green

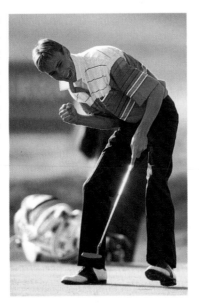

Australian Brett Ogle captures the leading individual prize at the first sudden-death hole

The winning putt: Davis Love seals it at the 72nd hole (above); Couples and Love (left) enjoy the spoils of victory

Couples and Johansson shooting 34s; Love and Forsbrand, 36s. On the back nine 'first class' became world class as the four players started hurling birdies (and one near-devastating eagle) at one another.

Couples birdied the 10th, 11th and 12th; Johansson, the 11th, 13th and 14th; Sweden took the lead for the very first time when Couples three-putted the 14th while Forsbrand birdied (his fourth in seven holes). Couples fought back by birdieing the 15th and 16th but when Johansson holed an amazing 40-foot putt for an eagle three at the 16th the anything-but-ice-cool Swedes were two ahead. Enter now Davis Love with a two at the short 17th: Sweden one ahead with one hole to play.

Only Forsbrand missed the green with his approach to the last but he managed to 'get up and down' for his par. Couples had hit a spectacular second to within two feet of the flag for a certain birdie (and a brilliant 65) and so all depended on the birdie attempts of both Love and Johansson. The American was at least 16 feet from the hole (and facing a very difficult putt) while the young Swede

was just five feet away. Surely a Swedish double now, or at least extra holes? But the Gods of La Moraleja chose to smile on a man called Love and not on the unfortunate Johansson. Davis holed, Per-Ulrik missed. He had equalled Couples' 65 yet was inconsolable. Valhalla for him; or as Shakespeare might have said, alas Per-Ulrik.

1992 WORLD CUP OF GOLF

FINAL · SCORES

USA	**548**					
F Couples	66	71	70	65	272	
D Love III	68	68	70	70	276	$120,000 each
SWEDEN	**549**					
A Forsbrand	68	66	68	70	272	
P-U Johansson	74	69	69	65	277	50,000 each
AUSTRALIA	**555**					
P O'Malley	72	71	73	69	285	
B Ogle	68	67	66	69	270	38,000 each
WALES	**555**					
I Woosnam	67	69	67	67	270	
M Mouland	72	70	71	72	285	38,000 each
GERMANY	**556**					
H P Thuel	75	73	65	70	283	
B Langer	71	66	66	70	273	25,000 each
SPAIN	**560**					
J Rivero	66	70	71	74	281	
M A Jimenez	70	70	69	70	279	20,000 each
N ZEALAND	**565**					
N Nobilo	71	67	69	67	274	
G J Turner	69	73	74	75	291	15,000 each
S AFRICA	**566**					
E Els	70	69	69	71	279	
D W Basson	70	74	77	66	287	12,000 each
ENGLAND	**569**					
D Gilford	74	70	72	70	285	
S Richardson	69	71	71	72	283	9,000 each
JAPAN	**571**					
K Murota	68	72	77	73	290	
H Miyase	71	70	71	69	281	8,000 each
CANADA	**572**					
R Zokol	71	70	72	75	288	
B Franklin	69	72	71	72	284	6,500 each
CHILE	**572**					
R Mackenzie	69	72	72	74	287	
G Encina A	71	73	67	74	285	6,500 each
PARAGUAY	**573**					
R Fretes	69	71	75	68	283	
C Franco	73	73	72	72	290	5,000 each
KOREA	**574**					
S Ho Choi	70	69	74	74	287	
N-S Park	70	71	73	73	287	4,000 each
ITALY	**575**					
S Grappasonni	74	74	73	67	288	
C Rocca	73	71	72	71	287	3,500 each

SCOTLAND	**576**					
G Brand Jnr	72	70	76	74	292	
C Montgomerie	71	73	74	66	284	3,500 each
IRELAND	**577**					
R Rafferty	77	70	72	73	292	
C O'Connor Jnr	73	72	71	69	285	3,500 each
SWITZERLAND	**577**					
P Quirici	68	72	71	70	281	
A Bossert	74	75	73	74	296	3,500 each
FRANCE	**578**					
M Besanceney	72	74	73	71	290	
J Van de Velde	73	74	71	70	288	3,500 each
MEXICO	**578**					
E Toledo	71	74	68	70	283	
E Serna	73	78	73	71	295	3,500 each
DENMARK	**580**					
O Eskildsen	75	71	74	72	292	
A Sorensen	73	74	69	72	288	3,500 each
TAIPEI	**581**					
Y S Hsieh	72	72	73	75	292	
T-C Wang	72	72	74	71	289	3,500 each
FINLAND	**587**					
A Kankkonen	76	73	76	73	298	
M Piltz	74	74	71	70	289	3,500 each
BRAZIL	**589**					
J Corteiz	76	79	73	75	303	
A J Pedro	72	73	74	67	286	3,500 each
ARGENTINA	**589**					
E Alvarez	69	68	71	81	289	
A Ortiz	76	72	74	78	300	3,500 each
PHILIPPINES	**590**					
R Pactolerin	81	78	74	73	306	
F Minoza	70	70	70	74	284	3,500 each

LEADING INDIVIDUAL SCORES

B Ogle	68	67	66	69	270	$75,000
I Woosnam	67	69	67	67	270	50,000
(Ogle won playoff at first extra hole)						
A Forsbrand	68	66	68	70	272	35,000
F Couples	66	71	70	65	272	35,000
B Langer	71	66	66	70	273	20,000
F Nobilo	71	67	69	67	274	15,000
D Love III	68	68	70	70	276	
P-U Johansson	74	69	69	65	277	
E Els	70	69	69	71	279	
M A Jimenez	70	70	69	70	279	
P Quirici	68	72	71	70	281	
H Miyase	71	70	71	69	281	
J Rivero	66	70	71	74	281	

4

GLOBAL GOLF

···

EUROPE

USA

AUSTRALASIA

JAPAN

REST OF THE WORLD

Heineken

WORLD
OF GOLF

EUROPE
· ·

DUNHILL
BRITISH MASTERS

HOLE	PLAYER	PAR	SCORE
16	JOHNSTONE		-17
17	O'CONNOR Jr		-17
17	FALDO		15
18	LUNA		
16	DAY		15
16	RICHARDSON		15
16	LANGER		
18	GILFORD		
17	LYLE		

O'CONNOR

1992 PGA EUROPEAN TOUR REVIEW

When an Englishman took the phrase 'Single European Market' far too literally...

Nick Faldo at Sunningdale during the European Open

On the same September day that Greg Norman finally ended his 30-month barren spell by winning the Canadian Open, 3000 miles away Nick Faldo gained his third successive European Tour victory at Sunningdale. And just as Greg won at Glen Abbey in his own, typically cavalier way (his final round was littered with eagles, birdies, pars, bogeys and double bogeys) so Nick won in his own, typically imperious way adding a 65 to earlier scores of 67-66-64.

The success at Sunningdale crowned a glorious summer for Faldo, a summer during which he captured his fifth Major championship at Muirfield, retained his Irish Open title at Killarney and thrilled his caddie by winning the Scandinavian Masters in Sweden. He hadn't finished either for the 'British' Open champion and the 'champion of Europe' went on to conquer the 'world' by adding the World Matchplay and World Championship trophies to his glittering 1992 cabinet. (Both are reviewed separately ahead.)

Nick even found time to lose a couple of tournaments on the European Tour as well, for he could, and perhaps should, have won the French and Belgian Open titles but for uncharacteristic lapses over the closing holes, and he came within two strokes of tieing the winning totals in the Spanish Open and the

'What are you staring at Mr Photographer!' Olazabal had a disappointing year by his standards

just want to go and die,' he said, in a state of near collapse soon after being given a blast of oxygen.) In sporadic bursts his form was brilliant, as it was, for instance, for the first two days of the World Matchplay, but by and large, 1992 is a year he will want to put behind him.

Ballesteros and Olazabal will also be hoping that the new year brings a change in their fortunes. Yet initially, Seve looked to

The Welsh Dragon: Woosnam smoked in 1992 but rarely caught fire

Benson and Hedges and British Masters events. Needless to say he smashed all existing Tour money records and was awarded the Vardon Trophy for achieving the lowest scoring average. A veritable *annus mirabilis*.

When one person is winning just about everything others must be 'losing' and of course it is no coincidence that Seve Ballesteros, José-Maria Olazabal and Ian Woosnam all had their least successful seasons for some time. Woosnam, number one in the Sony Rankings at the beginning of 1992, won only once all year - the Monte Carlo Open for the third year running - and his 1992 campaign got off to horrible start when he suffered a violent attack of food poisoning at the Asian Classic in Thailand. ('I

(Clockwise from the top) Spence, O'Malley, Singh and Fernandez: the Englishman, the Australian, the Fijian and the Argentinian: Europe's cosmopolitan winners - each of whom won in electrifying style

be picking up where he left off in 1991 (a year when he won five tournaments worldwide and comfortably picked up his sixth European Order of Merit title). In February he won the Dubai Classic, his 50th Tour victory; a week later became the first player to pass the £3 million winnings mark in Europe and in March he won the Majorcan Open. But then, just as Faldo started to string together a wonderful run of

Sluman in the second round and then, as if to rub salt into the wound, Faldo destroyed Sluman 8 and 7 in the final.

José-Maria's loss of form was not nearly as spectacular but his failure to add to two early successes was very mystifying. (In the spring he had won back to back tournaments, the Tenerife and Mediterranean Opens, the former with a stunning final round 63 that comprised nine pars and nine

American 'Long John' Daly flew to Europe and had a bash at the Italian Open

high finishes, Seve's form nose-dived dramatically. Between mid-March and mid-September Seve failed to finish in the top 25 in a single European tournament; in three of the events that Faldo won last year, the Open, the Scandinavian Masters, and the European Open, Seve missed the cut. Perhaps even more damaging to his pride however was the way he surrendered his World Matchplay title by losing to the American Jeff

birdies - 'I cannot possibly play better').

This is becoming depressing! Nineteen ninety-two was an exceptionally fine vintage in many respects and a celebratory year for many golfers. And it certainly wasn't all 'doom and gloom' for Spain: José Rivero had an excellent season; 45-year-old Canizares won the Roma Masters and there were first time wins for Miguel Martin and Miguel Jimenez.

The year's parade of champions was as cosmopolitan a collection as ever, with 38 Tour events producing winners from 15 different countries. (By contrast the 43 US tournaments in 1992 were won by players representing just five nations.) International stars regularly jetted in from all corners of the globe: even John Daly was spotted thundering 350-yard drives in Italy and Spain. Australian golfers didn't make nearly so big an impact in Europe as they had in 1991, with only Peter Senior and Peter O'Malley flying the flag. Zimbabwe's Tony Johnstone, however, had a memorable year, especially during an incredible month of May when he lost play-offs in the Benson and Hedges (to Senior) and British Masters (to O'Connor) but grabbed the important Volvo PGA Championship at Wentworth with a fourth round 65.

Several of the events were also won in extraordinary, and indeed sensational, style. Matthew Harris' superb picture of Christy O'Connor at Woburn in the British Masters

which opened this European chapter dramatically captures one such instance. The Irishman was in fact lucky to be playing at Woburn at all for only two weeks earlier he miraculously survived a helicopter crash. At Woburn he birdied six of his last eight holes, on more than one occasion despite wildly missing the fairway (he single putted each of the last eight greens!), to tie Tony Johnstone then hit his approach to within a few inches of the flag at the first play-off hole.

Argentinean Vicente Fernandez sank an 80-foot putt on the famous 18th green at The Belfry in the English Open then proceeded to leap and somersault across the grass like a six-year-old - quite a feat given that he was a 46-year-old, while Peter Mitchell chipped in for an eagle at the 72nd hole (and for his second 62 of the week) to win the Austrian Open in Salzburg.

Peter O'Malley didn't need any 80-foot putts or chip-ins to win the Scottish Open at Gleneagles but he did conclude his fourth round with scores of 2-3-2-3-3, or if you

Barry Lane peaked at precisely the right time in 1992

prefer, eagle-birdie-birdie-birdie-eagle! It was one of the great finishes of all time, yet incredibly seven weeks later Jamie Spence won the European Masters at Crans-sur-Sierre in equally brilliant fashion. Lying 10 shots behind overnight leader Colin Montgomerie, Spence fired a record 12 under par 60, playing his last five holes in six under par; Anders Forsbrand then birdied the 14th, 15th, 16th, 17th and 18th to tie Spence but the Englishman won the play-off with another birdie to register his first ever European victory. (I suppose if you are going to break your duck you may as well do it in style.)

If Spence's 60 was the greatest single round of the year in Europe (three others managed the same score but only Spence's was a 12 under par round), Vijay Singh's performance in the German Open was surely the most impressive over a full four days. Singh scored 66-68-64-64 for a superb 26 under par total and won by an extravagant 11 shots: it was a win comparable with Fred Couples' nine stroke success in last year's Bay Hill Classic.

Unlike Couples, the highly rated Fijian is not eligible of course to play in the 1993 Ryder Cup at The Belfry in September, an event which is certain to dominate 'Tour talk' throughout the 1993 season. Ryder Cup points began to be accumulated from last September, beginning at the European Masters (an extra, and deserved bonus, therefore fell to Spence that week). A second English golfer, Barry Lane, hit form at a choice time in this regard and with four top 10 finishes in successive events, culminating in a fine win in the German Masters, he ended the season heading Europe's Ryder Cup points table. So Lane should now make his debut at The Belfry, and following a brilliant year in 1992 it will be quite a surprise if

Anders Forsbrand doesn't do likewise. With Tour victories in Cannes and Florence (he also won the Equity & Law Challenge) plus a number of high finishes, Forsbrand at last did his abundant talent justice. Two other Swedes, Per-Ulrik Johansson and Robert Karlsson could also make the 12-man team; the former didn't play quite as well as in his 1991 rookie year but nearly won at The Belfry (of all places) where he was denied

Following a successful 1992 campaign, Anders Forsbrand should make the 1993 Ryder Cup team

only by Vicente's 80-footer, while the 6'4" Karlsson, largely unknown at the start of the season, lost a play-off to David Gilford in the Moroccan Open and might have won the European Open but for the imperious Faldo.

Aside from the Open champion, the two most consistent golfers in Europe last year were Bernhard Langer and Colin Montgomerie. Langer won twice - the Heineken Dutch Open (see ahead) and the Honda Open (his seventh Tour win on German soil) and came second on three

David Gilford led England to victory against Scotland in the Alfred Dunhill Cup at St Andrews

occasions, whereas Montgomerie had 11 top 10 finishes (only one fewer than Faldo) yet failed to win once.

If Montgomerie came close to becoming the luckiest golfer in the world in 1992 when he nearly captured the US Open title at windswept Pebble Beach, he succeeded in being the unluckiest golfer in Europe last year. In two of the above mentioned 'sensational finishes' - O'Malley's late blitz at Gleneagles and Spence's 60 at Crans - Montgomerie was the principal victim. Losing the Scottish Open naturally hurt him the most, especially as on the final day, sporting a navy sweater emblazoned with the cross of St Andrew he really did seem set to pull off a hugely popular home success. Nor could he have enjoyed the final day of the Alfred Dunhill Cup, for even though he didn't lose his own match he captained the Scottish team that was defeated by England.

Sandy Lyle also played in that event at St Andrews but, losing out to the Sassenachs excepted, he will have generally fond memories of 1992: in May he beat Montgomerie by one shot to win the Italian Open and in the last Tour event of the year, the prestigious Volvo Masters at Valderrama, he won for a second time following a sudden-death play-off. His vanquished opponent was you-know-who - no, not the mighty Faldo, but poor old Monty.

THE 1992 HEINEKEN DUTCH OPEN

● ●

I t was difficult to comprehend all that happened at Noordwijkse in the 1992 Heineken Dutch Open. First there were the great international celebrities who brought in the crowds and enlivened the proceedings: the American dandy in plus twos who breezed in determined to give his own special rendition of double-Dutch; the Great White Shark and the Dark Hyphenated Shark who surfaced from 'Down Under' and the dashing young Spaniard, who, for the first time in two years, missed out on the weekend party.

Then there were the characters who starred in an extraordinary final act: 19 putt-man from Wales; Hole-in-one man from Scotland; Creeper man from England - who won it, then lost it and the super cool German - an international celebrity in his own right - who lost it, then won it.

The cast were that cosmopolitan and the plot was that complicated.

Payne Stewart (right) was back to defend his title; (below) Greg Norman drives at Noordwijkse

Mike McLean thinks he's about to win the Heineken Dutch Open...

...Bernhard Langer is about to win the Heineken Dutch Open

The American donning the conspicuous golfing outfits was, of course, Payne Stewart, who returned to Noordwijkse last July and made a valiant attempt at retaining the title he had won in such brilliant fashion the previous year. The aquatically nick-named Australians, Greg Norman and Ian Baker-Finch headed a galaxy of international stars who were anxious to ensure that Stewart couldn't pull off a repeat of his incredible nine stroke victory.

Olazabal wasn't just the dashing young Spaniard but the pre-tournament favourite following his third place in the Open at Muirfield the previous week; it amazed everyone then when he failed to make the 36 hole cut and took Sandy Lyle with him.

Both Stewart and Norman featured prominently for three rounds, but neither played consistently well enough to win: the Australian opened with scores of 68 - 69 but then added 71 - 74 while the American, who achieved easily the best round of the week, an outstanding 63 on Saturday, also had a 75 on Friday.

After 36 holes Welsh golfer Mark Mouland was the surprise leader on 134, two ahead of Bernhard Langer and England's Mike McLean. If ever a player putted his way to the top of the leader board it was surely Mouland, for his second round 66 contained just 19 putts! - A European Tour record. Langer took over the lead in the third round, scoring a third consecutive sub 70 round and then charging through the field came Scotland's Gordon Brand Jnr.

Brand had a 67 in the third round, including a hole-in-one at the 6th and repeated his 67 on the final day to post an 11 under par target. Over the final holes it became clear that only Langer and McLean could equal - or better it. Langer did the former and watched as his playing partner, who earlier in the day had twice chipped-in, proceeded to sink a 25 foot birdie putt at the last to finish on 12 under par one ahead of Langer and Brand. Or so he thought.

McLean was ecstatic - but he had also, unintentionally, infringed a rule of golf. At the 11th McLean attempted to separate his ball from an entangling 40 foot creeper, something he thought he was entitled to do. In short he wasn't and the result was a two stroke penalty. Langer and Brand proceeded to play-off for the title which Langer cooly captured at the second sudden-death hole.

HEINEKEN DUTCH OPEN

Noordwijkse, 23 - 26 July

*Bernhard Langer	68	68	69	72	277	£100000
Gordon Brand Jnr.	72	71	67	67	277	66660
Gary Evans	70	67	71	70	278	33780
Mike McLean	69	67	70	72	278	33780
Derrick Cooper	73	68	68	70	279	23200
Payne Stewart	69	75	63	72	279	23200
Per-Ulrik Johansson	71	72	65	72	280	15480
Wayne Westner	71	71	68	70	280	15480
Mark Mouland	68	66	72	74	280	15480
Roger Winchester	68	71	69	73	281	10428
David Feherty	71	68	73	69	281	10428
Glen Day	71	68	72	70	281	10428
Greg J Turner	71	69	69	72	281	10428
Eamonn Darcy	71	66	73	71	281	10428
Vijay Singh	71	70	70	71	282	8112
Des Smyth	71	70	71	70	282	8112
Colin Montgomerie	71	69	71	71	282	8112
Greg Norman	68	69	71	74	282	8112
Miguel Angel Jimenez	72	72	68	70	282	8112
Peter O'Malley	72	71	68	72	283	6840
Jose Rivero	71	68	71	73	283	6840
De Wett Basson	72	70	70	71	283	6840
Anders Forsbrand	75	69	69	70	283	6840
Howard Clark	69	72	69	73	283	6840
Frank Nobilo	72	70	70	73	285	6210
Jean Van De Velde	71	71	69	74	285	6210

* Winner after playoff

Langer receives his prize: a handsome trophy and a cheque for £100,000

EUROPEAN TOUR RESULTS

30th January - 2nd February
JOHNNIE WALKER ASIAN CLASSIC
PINEHURST G & CC, BANGKOK, THAILAND

Ian Palmer	66	67	67	68	268	£83330
Brett Ogle	68	66	67	68	269	37283
Bernhard Langer	67	66	68	68	269	37283
Ronan Rafferty	67	68	69	65	269	37283
Mats Lanner	65	71	67	67	270	21200
Steven Richardson	63	70	69	69	271	17500
Peter Senior	67	71	67	67	272	15000
Mike McLean	67	69	66	71	273	11825
Paul Way	71	67	69	66	273	11825

6th - 9th February
DUBAI DESERT CLASSIC
EMIRATES GOLF CLUB, DUBAI

* Seve Ballesteros	66	67	69	70	272	£58330
Ronan Rafferty	66	70	67	69	272	38880
David Feherty	69	69	68	69	275	19705
Mark James	67	68	71	69	275	19705
Nick Faldo	70	68	69	69	276	14830
Mike McLean	67	71	68	71	277	9830
Ian Woosnam	70	67	70	70	277	9830
Isao Aoki	68	69	73	67	277	9830
Barry Lane	69	69	72	67	277	9830
Jorge Berendt	70	70	69	69	278	7000

13th - 16th February
TURESPANA MASTERS OPEN DE ANDALUCIA
PARADORES CLUB DE CAMPO, DE MALAGA

Vijay Singh	72	70	69	66	277	£50000
Gary Evans	73	69	65	72	279	33330
Andrew Hare	75	70	66	70	281	16890
Anders Forsbrand	71	70	69	71	281	16890
Jay Townsend	75	69	69	69	282	12700
Mike McLean	68	72	72	71	283	10500
Marc Farry	73	75	68	68	284	8250
José Maria Canizares	75	72	68	69	284	8250
Paul Broadhurst	75	72	71	67	285	6690

20th - 23rd February
TURESPANA OPEN DE TENERIFE
GOLF DEL SUR, TENERIFE

José Maria Olazabal	71	68	66	63	268	£50000
Miguel Angel Martin	69	68	67	69	273	33330
Jose Rivero	75	72	69	64	280	16890
Mike McLean	71	70	67	72	280	16890
Joakim Haeggman	74	71	69	67	281	10733
Stephen Field	73	72	67	69	281	10733
James Spence	72	72	67	70	281	10733
Gary Evans	71	68	72	71	282	7095
Philip Walton	77	70	68	67	282	7095

27th February - 1st March
OPEN MEDITERRANIA
EL BOSQUE GOLF & COUNTRY CLUB, VALENCIA

José Maria Olazabal	68	71	69	68	276	£66660
Jose Rivero	69	68	69	72	278	44440
Joakim Haeggman	70	69	72	68	279	25040
Costantino Rocca	73	70	67	70	280	16980
Vijay Singh	70	67	71	72	280	16980
Brett Ogle	69	71	71	69	280	16980
Alberto Binaghi	70	71	67	73	281	12000
Christy O'Connor Jnr	74	67	67	74	282	9460
James Spence	72	68	70	72	282	9460

5th - 8th March
TURESPANA OPEN DE BALEARES
SANTA PONSA

* Seve Ballesteros	70	70	69	68	277	£41660
Jesper Parnevik	70	72	67	68	277	27770
Vicente Fernandez	69	70	71	69	279	15650
Jose Rivero	70	73	68	69	280	11550
Santiago Luna	69	70	71	70	280	11550
Eduardo Romero	70	71	70	70	281	7500
Gordon Brand Jnr	68	66	74	73	281	7500
Barry Lane	67	71	70	73	281	7500

* denotes winner in play-off

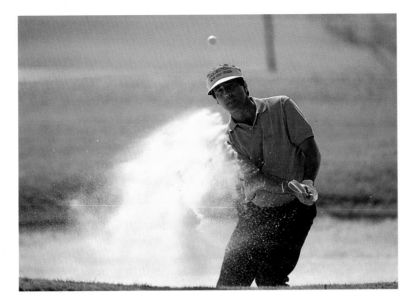

Seve Ballesteros
enjoyed early
successes in
Dubai and
Majorca – then
the wheels
came off

11th - 14th March
OPEN CATALONIA
MAS NOU, GIRONA

Jose Rivero	70	71	72	67	280	£50000
Haydn Selby-Green	72	73	66	70	281	22370
José Maria Canizares	74	73	67	67	281	22370
Johan Rystrom	68	76	70	67	281	22370
Anders Forsbrand	72	73	67	71	283	10733
José Maria Olazabal	74	69	69	71	283	10733
Mats Lanner	74	68	69	72	283	10733
Paul Broadhurst	76	69	71	68	284	6730
Magnus Sunesson	69	71	73	71	284	6730
Darren Clarke	68	75	72	69	284	6730

18th - 22nd March
PORTUGUESE OPEN
VILA SOL, VILAMOURA

Ronan Rafferty	67	71	67	68	273	£37500
Anders Forsbrand	69	67	68	70	274	25000
Peter Senior	74	64	68	70	276	14070
Sam Torrance	70	67	71	69	277	9533
José Maria Canizares	75	69	62	71	277	9533
Juan Quiros	69	65	74	69	277	9533
Barry Lane	71	68	72	67	278	6150
Gordon J Brand	68	73	71	66	278	6150
David Gilford	73	69	70	67	279	5010

26th - 29th March
VOLVO OPEN DI FIRENZE
GOLF DEL' UGOLINO, FLORENCE

Anders Forsbrand	69	69	67	66	271	£37500
Peter Senior	69	66	68	69	272	25000
Martin Gates	73	65	66	71	275	14070
David Gilford	72	67	68	69	276	10375
Jorge Berendt	70	68	71	67	276	10375
Ricky Willison	75	67	67	68	277	6716
Eduardo Romero	73	70	69	65	277	6716
Peter Mitchell	68	68	69	72	277	6716
Des Smyth	73	68	68	69	278	4530
Steven Richardson	70	67	72	69	278	4530
Paul Lawrie	68	67	76	67	278	4530

2nd - 5th April
ROMA MASTERS
CASTELGANDOLFO

* José Maria Canizares	72	71	69	74	286	£37500
Barry Lane	72	72	76	66	286	25000
James Payne	70	73	77	69	289	14070
Mark Roe	68	76	75	72	291	9533
Paul Curry	72	71	75	73	291	9533
Eduardo Romero	71	75	72	73	291	9533
Anders Forsbrand	73	75	77	67	292	6150
Bill Longmuir	70	72	75	75	292	6150

9th - 12th April
JERSEY EUROPEAN AIRWAYS OPEN
LA MOYE, JERSEY

Daniel Silva	69	65	70	73	277	£37500
Chris Moody	69	71	70	69	279	25000
Robert Karlsson	70	67	70	74	281	11606
Mark Roe	69	65	68	79	281	11606
Peter Mitchell	72	67	65	77	281	11606
David Gilford	69	67	69	77	282	5375
David J Russell	69	71	70	72	282	5375
Heinz P Thuel	70	69	70	73	282	5375
Mark James	67	69	70	76	282	5375
Paul Broadhurst	70	72	68	72	282	5375
Barry Lane	66	71	71	74	282	5375
Martin Gates	70	70	69	73	282	5375

16th - 19th April
MOROCCAN OPEN
ROYAL DAR-ES-SALAM, RABAT

* David Gilford	76	73	68	70	287	£41660
Robert Karlsson	70	75	72	70	287	27770
Ricky Willison	70	75	73	71	289	15650
Mats Hallberg	71	75	73	71	290	11550
Darren Clarke	74	75	70	71	290	11550
Steven Bowman	71	73	74	73	291	7025
Fredrik Lindgren	68	74	76	73	291	7025
Anders Forsbrand	70	78	71	72	291	7025
Gordon Manson	74	72	73	72	291	7025

23rd - 26th April
CREDIT LYONNAIS CANNES OPEN
CANNES MOUGINS

Anders Forsbrand	65	70	68	70	273	£58330
Per-Ulrik Johansson	66	69	69	70	274	38880
Colin Montgomerie	70	69	68	69	276	21910
Vijay Singh	67	75	70	66	278	17500
Ian Woosnam	74	68	72	66	280	12526
Tony Johnstone	69	72	77	62	280	12526
Peter Teravainen	69	69	71	71	280	12526
Robert Karlsson	71	69	70	72	282	8750

30th April - 3rd May
LANCIA MARTINI ITALIAN OPEN
MONTICELLO

Sandy Lyle	66	71	65	68	270	£61038
Colin Montgomerie	67	70	68	66	271	40652
Paul Way	69	69	66	68	272	20621
Mark O'Meara	72	65	68	67	272	20621
Vijay Singh	71	68	69	68	276	15525
Frank Nobilo	73	68	69	68	278	10988
Jose Rivero	71	70	69	68	278	10988
Eduardo Romero	70	72	71	65	278	10988

7th - 10th May
BENSON AND HEDGES INTERNATIONAL OPEN
ST MELLION GOLF & COUNTRY CLUB, NR SALTASH, CORNWALL

* Peter Senior	74	73	70	70	287	£83330
Tony Johnstone	71	73	74	69	287	55550
Nick Faldo	71	72	76	69	288	28150
Jim Payne	72	70	75	71	288	28150
Anders Forsbrand	68	77	72	72	289	21200
Paul Curry	72	73	75	70	290	17500
Craig Parry	67	76	73	75	291	15000
Santiago Luna	71	78	72	71	292	11825
Philip Walton	71	76	75	70	292	11825
Bernhard Langer	71	74	73	75	293	9595
Mats Lanner	69	73	74	77	293	9595

14th - 17th May
PEUGEOT SPANISH OPEN
REAL AUTOMOVIL CLUB DE ESPANA (R.A.C.E.), MADRID

Andrew Sherborne	71	66	63	71	271	£66660
Nick Faldo	70	70	66	66	272	44440
Justin Hobday	72	66	71	66	275	25040
Eduardo Romero	67	68	70	71	276	16980
Santiago Luna	69	64	72	71	276	16980
Jose Rivero	74	67	63	72	276	16980
Miguel Angel Jimenez	66	69	72	70	277	12000
Steven Richardson	65	74	71	68	278	9460
Eamonn Darcy	71	68	72	67	278	9460
José Maria Olazabal	70	69	69	71	279	7680
Steven Bowman	71	70	71	67	279	7680

22nd - 25th May
VOLVO PGA CHAMPIONSHIP
WENTWORTH CLUB, WEST COURSE

Tony Johnstone	67	70	70	65	272	£100000
Gordon Brand Jnr.	67	70	68	69	274	52110
José Maria Olazabal	71	70	67	66	274	52110
Magnus Sunesson	72	68	64	71	275	27700
Gary Evans	74	66	66	69	275	27700
David Gilford	64	73	71	68	276	19500
José Maria Canizares	70	72	66	68	276	19500
Nick Faldo	70	68	69	70	277	15000
Johan Rystrom	69	69	72	68	278	13440
Colin Montgomerie	70	72	67	70	279	10428
Paul Way	71	69	68	71	279	10428
Peter Senior	67	69	74	69	279	10428
James Spence	67	66	75	71	279	10428
Eduardo Romero	70	70	69	70	279	10428

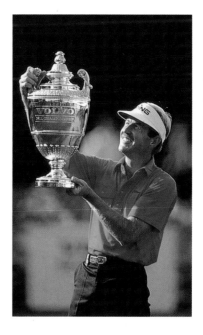

Tony Johnstone was a popular winner of the Volvo PGA Championship at Wentworth

28th - 31st May
DUNHILL BRITISH MASTERS
WOBURN GOLF & COUNTRY CLUB

* Christy O'Connor Jnr.	71	67	66	66	270	£100000
Tony Johnstone	69	67	65	69	270	66660
Steven Richardson	67	66	69	69	271	37560
Nick Faldo	68	68	69	67	272	30000
Glen Day	68	65	69	71	273	21466
Bernhard Langer	67	65	70	71	273	21466
Santiago Luna	70	70	65	68	273	21466
Sandy Lyle	71	66	69	68	274	15000
David Gilford	73	65	69	68	275	13440
Eduardo Romero	71	71	68	66	276	12000
Ernie Els	69	70	71	67	277	10660
Paul Broadhurst	72	67	69	69	277	10660

4th - 7th June
CARROLLS IRISH OPEN
KILLARNEY GOLF AND FISHING CLUB

* Nick Faldo	66	65	68	75	274	£76274
Wayne Westner	68	70	68	68	274	50846
Paul Broadhurst	68	68	67	73	272	28649
Anders Forsbrand	71	68	70	69	278	21144
Colin Montgomerie	72	66	68	72	278	21144
Paul Lawrie	69	74	66	70	279	14874
Bernhard Langer	67	72	70	70	279	14874
Sam Torrance	74	72	67	67	280	11441
Jeff Hawkes	74	72	67	68	281	10205
Malcolm Mackenzie	72	66	72	74	284	9153

Nick Faldo in reflective mood during The Carrolls Irish Open at Killarney

11th - 14th June
MITSUBISHI AUSTRIAN OPEN
GUT ALTENTANN GOLF & COUNTRY CLUB, SALZBURG

Peter Mitchell	74	62	73	62	271	£58330
James Spence	68	71	70	63	272	26096
David J Russell	66	72	69	65	272	26096
Peter Fowler	70	69	67	66	272	26096
Barry Lane	67	74	68	67	276	13540
Ole Eskildsen	69	68	71	68	276	13540
Per-Ulrik Johansson	66	68	71	72	277	9625
Jean Van De Velde	68	66	72	71	277	9625
Jose Manuel Carriles	70	69	72	67	278	7820

18th - 21st June
OPEN DE LYON
LYON GOLF CLUB, VILLETTE-D'ANTHON

David J Russell	68	66	67	66	267	£37500
Brett Ogle	69	72	68	64	272	25000
Jay Townsend	67	74	68	65	274	12660
Paul Broadhurst	66	72	69	67	274	12660
Robert Karlsson	64	71	72	68	275	8675
Carl Mason	70	70	68	67	275	8675
Gavin Levenson	71	69	66	70	276	6150
Grant Waite	69	71	65	71	276	6150

25th - 28th June
PEUGEOT FRENCH OPEN
NATIONAL GOLF CLUB, PARIS

Miguel Angel Martin	70	71	66	69	276	£66660
Martin Poxon	72	68	73	65	278	44440
Costantino Rocca	69	73	72	66	280	22520
Nick Faldo	71	70	65	74	280	22520
Peter Baker	70	69	70	72	281	16940
John McHenry	67	71	72	72	282	10584
Sandy Lyle	71	74	66	71	282	10584
Peter Smith	71	70	70	71	282	10584
Anders Forsbrand	73	72	67	70	282	10584
Vicente Fernandez	68	73	72	69	282	10584
Glen Day	74	68	66	75	283	7360
Stephen Field	70	74	72	68	284	5810

1st - 4th July
THE EUROPEAN MONTE CARLO GOLF OPEN
MONT AGEL GOLF CLUB, LA TURBIE, MONTE CARLO

Ian Woosnam	66	65	66	64	261	£73474
Johan Rystrom	70	64	69	60	263	38281
Mark McNulty	67	67	66	63	263	38281
Darren Clarke	66	60	73	65	264	22051
Eduardo Romero	67	66	65	68	266	18699
Jonathan Sewell	67	68	68	66	269	13230
Paul McGinley	65	66	69	69	269	13230
Anders Forsbrand	73	67	65	64	269	13230

8th - 11th July
BELL'S SCOTTISH OPEN
GLENEAGLES HOTEL (KING'S COURSE)

Peter O'Malley	65	70	65	62	262	£100000
Colin Montgomerie	65	64	70	65	264	66660
Nick Faldo	69	62	69	65	265	33780
Mark McNulty	68	68	66	63	265	33780
Bernhard Langer	62	67	67	70	266	25400
Mats Lanner	64	69	66	68	267	21000
Craig Parry	67	69	66	67	269	15480
Costantino Rocca	70	66	68	65	269	15480
Ian Woosnam	66	66	70	67	269	15480
Rodger Davis	70	65	67	69	271	10740
Philip Walton	66	70	65	70	271	10740
James Spence	65	67	69	70	271	10740
Peter Senior	66	63	72	70	271	10740

30th July - 2nd August
SCANDINAVIAN MASTERS
BARSEBACK, SWEDEN

Nick Faldo	70	72	66	69	277	£100000
Danny Mijovic	72	70	69	69	280	33103
Frank Nobilo	72	70	68	70	280	33103
Robert Allenby	71	71	70	68	280	33103
Peter Baker	72	69	70	69	280	33103
José Maria Olazabal	72	67	72	69	280	33103
Peter O'Malley	71	70	68	71	280	33103
James Spence	70	72	68	71	281	13480
Per-Ulrik Johansson	70	70	73	68	281	13480
Stephen Field	70	74	68	69	281	13480

Patriotism rules: Colin Montgomerie did everything but win the Scottish Open at Gleneagles

6th - 9th August
BMW INTERNATIONAL OPEN
GOLFPLATZ MUNCHEN NORD-EICHENRIED, MUNICH

* Paul Azinger	66	67	66	67	266	£83330
Glen Day	66	70	65	65	266	33262
Bernhard Langer	66	69	65	66	266	33262
Anders Forsbrand	68	65	66	67	266	33262
Mark James	69	66	67	64	266	33262
Colin Montgomerie	65	67	72	64	268	16250
Steen Tinning	70	62	70	66	268	16250
Sandy Lyle	70	67	65	67	269	12500
Costantino Rocca	65	69	66	70	270	9394
Frank Nobilo	68	68	71	63	270	9394
Ross McFarlane	67	68	67	68	270	9394
Stephen McAllister	70	66	67	67	270	9394
Darren Clarke	68	62	71	69	270	9394

20th - 23rd August
VOLVO GERMAN OPEN
HUBBELRATH, DUSSELDORF

Vijay Singh	66	68	64	64	262	£87500
Jose Manuel Carriles	69	69	67	68	273	58275

Wayne Grady	70	71	64	69	274	32850
Ian Woosnam	67	65	73	70	275	26250
Malcolm Mackenzie	68	69	69	70	276	20317
Frank Nobilo	65	71	71	69	276	20317
Andrew Sherborne	71	68	69	69	277	15750
Marc Farry	69	69	71	69	278	11265
Eduardo Romero	69	66	71	72	278	11265
Peter O'Malley	68	68	69	73	278	11265
John Hawksworth	66	69	71	72	278	11265

28th - 31st August
MURPHY'S ENGLISH OPEN
THE BELFRY (BRABAZON COURSE)

Vicente Fernandez	69	72	73	69	283	£91660
Fredrik Lindgren	69	68	74	73	284	47765
Per-Ulrik Johansson	71	68	72	73	284	47765
Barry Lane	70	69	78	68	285	27500
Mark Roe	69	69	75	73	286	21275
Brett Ogle	72	67	75	72	286	21275
Silvio Grappasonni	70	69	74	74	287	15125
Keith Waters	71	69	76	71	287	15125
Santiago Luna	73	71	74	70	288	12280

3rd - 6th September
CANON EUROPEAN MASTERS
CRANS-SUR-SIERRE, SWITZERLAND

* James Spence	67	71	73	60	271	£93859
Anders Forsbrand	68	70	68	65	271	62535
Colin Montgomerie	63	70	68	71	272	35267
Sandy Lyle	71	70	66	67	274	28169
Sven Struver	68	72	67	68	275	20169
Jose Rivero	64	73	69	69	275	20169
Per-Ulrik Johansson	68	68	74	65	275	20169
Jim Payne	69	72	72	63	276	14084
Robert Lee	69	71	70	67	277	11943
Mats Lanner	68	68	70	71	277	11943

10th - 13th September
GA EUROPEAN OPEN
SUNNINGDALE (OLD COURSE)

Nick Faldo	67	66	64	65	262	£100000
Robert Karlsson	64	67	67	67	265	66660
Mark James	64	68	69	65	266	37560
Barry Lane	66	68	69	68	271	27700
José Maria Olazabal	70	67	69	65	271	27700
Steven Richardson	68	71	66	67	272	21000
Mats Lanner	65	68	71	69	273	16500
Jose Rivero	68	69	69	67	273	16500
Ian Palmer	63	74	69	68	274	11280
Philip Walton	66	71	69	68	274	11280
Frank Nobilo	64	72	70	68	274	11280
James Spence	69	67	67	71	274	11280

17th - 20th September
TROPHEE LANCOME
ST-NOM-LA-BRETECHE, FRANCE

Mark Roe	67	69	66	65	267	£79000
Vicente Fernandez	66	70	69	64	269	52700
Eduardo Romero	66	67	69	68	270	24700
Jim Payne	69	68	65	68	270	24700
Steven Richardson	68	68	71	63	270	24700
José Maria Olazabal	65	69	68	69	271	16800
Peter Senior	69	66	66	71	272	14300
Barry Lane	66	69	68	70	273	11250
Tony Johnstone	67	67	69	70	273	11250

Jamie Spence	72	67	68	67	274	8455
Peter Mitchell	71	65	68	70	274	8455
Christy O'Connor Jnr	70	67	68	69	274	8455
Ian Woosnam	66	68	76	64	274	8455

24th - 27th September
THE PIAGET OPEN
ROYAL ZOUTE GOLF CLUB, BELGIUM

Miguel Angel Jimenez	71	70	64	69	274	£100000
Barry Lane	68	68	71	70	277	66660
Seve Ballesteros	70	71	70	67	278	33780
Torsten Giedeon	72	70	71	65	278	33780
Per-Ulrik Johansson	72	69	69	69	279	19850
Ian Woosnam	67	70	71	71	279	19850
Nick Faldo	69	67	69	74	279	19850
Sandy Lyle	69	70	72	68	279	19850

1st - 4th October
MERCEDES GERMAN MASTERS
STUTTGARTER, MONSHEIM

Barry Lane	71	67	66	68	272	£100000
Rodger Davis	67	69	69	69	274	44740
Bernhard Langer	65	71	68	70	274	44740
Ian Woosnam	68	68	66	72	274	44740
Costantino Rocca	65	69	68	73	275	23200
Steven Richardson	70	71	68	66	275	23200
Paul Broadhurst	67	68	73	68	276	16500
Christy O'Connor Jnr	67	66	72	71	276	16500
Chris Moody	69	70	70	68	277	12720
Miguel Angel Jimenez	67	71	69	70	277	12720

8th - 11th October
HONDA OPEN
GUT KADEN, HAMBURG, GERMANY

Bernhard Langer	69	65	70	69	273	£75000
Darren Clarke	71	69	67	69	276	50000
Roger Chapman	72	65	72	69	278	28170
Russell Claydon	68	77	68	66	279	22500
Mark Roe	70	71	70	69	280	17405
Fred Couples	69	70	70	71	280	17405
Wayne Westner	72	70	66	73	281	11600
Ernie Els	71	70	71	69	281	11600
Sven Struver	74	72	71	64	281	11600

October 15 - 18
ALFRED DUNHILL CUP
OLD COURSE, ST ANDREWS, SCOTLAND

Round Robin Event

GROUP ONE		GROUP TWO	
Final table	Points	Final table	Points
USA	2	England	2
Ireland	2	Spain	2
New Zealand	2	Japan	1
Korea	0	Italy	1

GROUP THREE		GROUP FOUR	
Final table	Points	Final table	Points
Scotland	2	Australia	3
Canada	2	Germany	2
Sweden	2	South Africa	1
France	0	Thailand	0

SEMI-FINALS

England beat USA 2-1 Gilford (69) bt. Couples (70)
Richardson (68) bt. Love III (71) Spence (72) lost to Kite (71)
Scotland beat Australia 2-1
Montgomerie (68) bt. Baker-Finch (72) Lyle (69) bt. Davis (73)
Brand Jnr (73) lost to Norman (68)
USA and Australia received £95,000, £31,666 per man
Leading Individual Scorer: Greg Norman (Aus)

FINAL

England beat Scotland 2-0
Richardson (71) bt. Brand Jnr (73) Spence (69) tied with
Montgomerie (69) Gilford (71) bt. Lyle (74)
England received £300,000, £100,000 per man
Scotland received £150,000, £50,000 per man

22nd - 25th October
IBERIA MADRID OPEN
REAL CLUB DE LA PUERTA DE HIERRO, MADRID

David Feherty	71	65	69	67	272	£66660
Mark McNulty	66	71	66	73	276	44440
Eamonn Darcy	68	69	72	69	278	18995
Eduardo Romero	74	67	68	69	278	18995
Colin Montgomerie	66	69	73	70	278	18995
Ronan Rafferty	71	67	70	70	278	18995
Derrick Cooper	72	72	67	68	279	8860
Vijay Singh	71	69	70	69	279	8860

29th October - 1st November
VOLVO MASTERS
VALDERRAMA, SOTOGRANDE, SPAIN

* Sandy Lyle	72	70	72	73	287	£110000
Colin Montgomerie	76	70	72	69	287	73330
Christy O'Connor Jnr	76	68	71	74	289	41310
Eduardo Romero	74	72	70	74	290	30660
Tony Johnstone	78	68	70	74	290	30660
José-Maria Olazabal	75	72	73	71	291	22000
Brett Ogle	77	72	72	70	291	22000
Bernhard Langer	72	76	70	74	292	16135
Gordon Brand Jnr	70	74	76	72	292	16135
Peter Mitchell	73	73	76	71	293	12670
Glen Day	78	71	72	72	293	12670
Miguel Angel Jimenez	73	72	76	72	293	12670

Sandy Lyle at Valderrama during the Volvo Masters

1992 PGA EUROPEAN TOUR WINNERS SUMMARY

January	JOHNNIE WALKER ASIAN CLASSIC	Ian Palmer (SA)
February	DUBAI DESERT CLASSIC	Seve Ballesteros (Sp)
	TURESPANA MASTERS - OPEN DE ANDALUCIA	Vijay Singh (Fij)
	TURESPANA OPEN DE TENERIFE	José-Maria Olazabal (Sp)
	OPEN MEDITERRANIA	José-Maria Olazabal (Sp)
March	TURESPANA OPEN DE BALEARES	Seve Ballesteros (Sp)
	OPEN CATALONIA	Jose Rivero (Sp)
	PORTUGUESE OPEN	Ronan Rafferty (N.Ire)
	VOLVO OPEN DI FIRENZE	Anders Forsbrand (Swe)
April	ROMA MASTERS	José-Maria Canizares (Sp)
	JERSEY EUROPEAN AIRWAYS OPEN	Daniel Silva (Port)
	MOROCCAN OPEN	David Gilford (Eng)
	CREDIT LYONNAIS CANNES OPEN	Anders Forsbrand (Swe)
	LANCIA MARTINI ITALIAN OPEN	Sandy Lyle (Scot)
May	BENSON AND HEDGES INTERNATIONAL OPEN	Peter Senior (Aus)
	PEUGEOT SPANISH OPEN	Andrew Sherborne (Eng)
	VOLVO PGA CHAMPIONSHIP	Tony Johnstone (Zim)
	DUNHILL BRITISH MASTERS	Christy O'Connor Jnr (Ire)
June	CARROLLS IRISH OPEN	Nick Faldo (Eng)
	MITSUBISHI AUSTRIAN OPEN	Peter Mitchell (Eng)
	OPEN DE LYON TROPHEE V33	David J Russell (Eng)
	PEUGEOT FRENCH OPEN	Miguel Angel Martin (Sp)
July	THE EUROPEAN MONTE CARLO GOLF OPEN	Ian Woosnam (Wal)
	BELL'S SCOTTISH OPEN	Peter O'Malley (Aus)
	121ST OPEN CHAMPIONSHIP	Nick Faldo (Eng)
	HEINEKEN DUTCH OPEN	Bernhard Langer (Ger)
	SCANDINAVIAN MASTERS	Nick Faldo (Eng)
August	BMW INTERNATIONAL OPEN	Paul Azinger (USA)
	VOLVO GERMAN OPEN	Vijay Singh (Fij)
	MURPHY'S ENGLISH OPEN	Vicente Fernandez (Arg)
September	CANON EUROPEAN MASTERS	Jamie Spence (Eng)
	GA EUROPEAN OPEN	Nick Faldo (Eng)
	* EQUITY & LAW CHALLENGE	Anders Forsbrand (Swe)
	TROPHEE LANCOME	Mark Roe (Eng)
	PIAGET OPEN	Miguel Angel Jimenez (Sp)
October	MERCEDES GERMAN MASTERS	Barry Lane (Eng)
	HONDA OPEN	Bernhard Langer (Ger)
	* TOYOTA WORLD MATCHPLAY CHAMPIONSHIP	Nick Faldo (Eng)
	* ALFRED DUNHILL CUP	England
	* UAP EUROPEAN UNDER 25 CHAMPIONSHIP	Paul Lawrie (Scot)
	IBERIA MADRID OPEN	David Feherty (N.Ire)
	VOLVO MASTERS	Sandy Lyle (Scot)

* PGA European Tour Approved Special Event

1992 PGA
EUROPEAN TOUR

VOLVO ORDER OF MERIT: TOP 100

**Nick Faldo adopts an
all-too-familiar pose**

1	Nick Faldo	£708,522							
2	Bernhard Langer	488,912							
3	Colin Montgomerie	444,712							
4	Anders Forsbrand	417,471							
5	Barry Lane	394,251							
6	José-Maria Olazabal	385,626							
7	Tony Johnstone	340,917							
8	Sandy Lyle	333,141							
9	Vijay Singh	293,736							
10	Jamie Spence	287,956							
11	Ian Woosnam	281,406				66	Martin Poxon	76,949
12	Jose Rivero	268,873	39	Santiago Luna	143,064	67	Paul Curry	75,533
13	Gordon Brand Jnr	247,115	40	Mike McLean	140,903	68	Jay Townsend	72,849
14	Miguel Angel Jimenez	229,239	41	Darren Clarke	140,294	69	Daniel Silva	72,470
15	Peter Senior	226,204	42	Paul Broadhurst	138,731	70	Derrick Cooper	72,406
16	Vicente Fernandez	215,849	43	Malcolm Mackenzie	135,970	71	Stephen Field	71,783
17	Per-Ulrik Johansson	213,283	44	Mats Lanner	135,427	72	Magnus Sunesson	70,123
18	Mark Roe	209,658	45	Ian Palmer	129,447	73	Jesper Parnevik	68,828
19	Steven Richardson	204,892	46	David Feherty	125,688	74	Stephen McAllister	68,073
20	Eduardo Romero	199,506	47	Wayne Westner	122,143	75	Ernie Els	66,625
21	Peter O'Malley	199,076	48	Rodger Davis	121,169	76	Des Smyth	65,961
22	Robert Karlsson	196,577	49	Joakim Haeggman	111,351	77	Silvio Grappasonni	64,122
23	Christy O'Connor Jnr	194,033	50	Peter Baker	110,075	78	Gordon J Brand	59,763
24	David Gilford	192,898	51	David J Russell	109,267	79	Mats Hallberg	59,179
25	Peter Mitchell	183,777	52	Johan Rystrom	105,726	80	Anders Sorensen	56,930
26	Ronan Rafferty	176,860	53	Philip Walton	105,364	81	Richard Boxall	56,084
27	Costantino Rocca	175,091	54	Paul Way	104,668	82	Howard Clark	55,987
28	Severiano Ballesteros	172,052	55	Danny Mijovic	95,620	83	Paul Lawrie	55,730
29	Brett Ogle	154,536	56	Fredrik Lindgren	95,597	84	Mark Mouland	53,974
30	Andrew Sherborne	154,421	57	Jose Carriles	94,115	85	Steen Tinning	53,836
31	Frank Nobilo	152,403	58	Russell Claydon	93,318	86	Robert Allenby	53,431
32	Mark James	152,300	59	Eamonn Darcy	93,255	87	Jonathan Sewell	52,745
33	Jim Payne	148,352	60	Roger Chapman	86,450	88	Peter Teravainen	51,714
34	Mark McNulty	146,381	61	Carl Mason	85,616	89	Gavin Levenson	49,564
35	Gary Evans	146,246	62	Sam Torrance	84,487	90	Patrick Hall	49,535
36	Glen Day	144,547	63	Peter Fowler	83,445	91	Marc Farry	48,049
37	José-Maria Canizares	144,469	64	Jean Van de Velde	82,176	92	Justin Hobday	47,247
38	Miguel Angel Martin	144,370	65	Chris Moody	80,931	93	Martin Gates	47,184
						94	Jon Robson	46,470
						95	Roger Winchester	46,211
						96	Phillip Price	45,631
						97	Paul McGinley	44,761
						98	Greg J Turner	44,468
						99	Keith Waters	44,189
						100	Robert Lee	43,775

THE WORLD MATCHPLAY CHAMPIONSHIP

The King is dead. Long live the King...

There would be no record sixth win for Seve Ballesteros in 1992

Some things in golf, as in life, never change: one is the golden glory of Wentworth in Autumn; another is the eagerness with which enthusiasts await the annual World Matchplay Championship. On the other side of the Royal and Ancient coin there is 'form'; for even among the finest exponents of the game it is anything but permanent. It can, for instance, erode (or build) gradually over 12 months and it can sometimes suddenly vanish (or appear) overnight. The 1992 World Matchplay Championship at Wentworth was all about form.

Twelve months earlier Ballesteros was the king: he achieved a record-equalling fifth win in the championship and increased his tally of victories for the year to five; in the final he gave Nick Price a lesson in brilliance and dished a couple Americans en route - Fred Couples being one of them. Yet as Price and Couples went on to enjoy their finest ever seasons in 1992, Seve arrived at Wentworth in the midst of his worst ever slump. Even the most cursory of glances at the 1992 record book revealed that the man to beat at Wentworth was not Seve but Nick Faldo, yet for two days it looked as if a third player, Ian Woosnam, who had won precious little all year but had now suddenly discovered such a rich vein of form, would sweep everyone aside and claim a third victory in the event.

Despite being the champion in 1987 and 1990, Woosnam was not one of the seeded players for the 1992 event (Faldo, Price,

Olazabal and Ballesteros were) and so had to play in the first round. This was also the case with three-time winner Greg Norman who at long last appeared to be emerging from his own prolonged slump. On the Thursday the two were matched against Japanese golfer Norio Suzuki and Brad Faxon, twice a winner on the '92 US Tour. As many had anticipated, Norman's game with the American was much the closer and he in fact only just scraped through on the final hole, while Woosnam's was a very one sided contest. Suzuki didn't play particularly poorly but the Welshman produced a barrage of birdies to win 8 and 6. In the other first round matches, Ryder Cup player Mark O'Meara defeated probable-future-Ryder Cup player Anders Forsbrand at the 37th and Jeff Sluman beat Vijay Singh 4 and 3. With Wentworth 'playing long' the big-hitting Fijian had fancied his chances against 5' 7" Sluman, but the American produced a 67 in the morning and frankly, that was that.

Sluman's reward was a quarter-final match against the defending champion. It was a game that Ballesteros really should have won, for though there were very few glimpses of the Spaniard's genius he found himself one up with five to play, but still managed to lose by two holes. Watching him thrashing about in the woodland 50 yards short and right of the 18th green was not a pretty sight, especially as it was close to the spot where he once chipped-in for a miraculous eagle against Arnold Palmer.

The Sluman-Ballesteros game was the only close encounter of the day: Nick Faldo made his first appearance in the championship and almost nonchalantly dispatched Mark O'Meara 5 and 3; Nick Price and Greg Norman drove off soon after breakfast but were back in the clubhouse in time for morning coffee when the Australian

was forced to retire with a cricked neck and Olazabal's return to Wentworth (there had been much fuss in 1991 when he wasn't invited despite being number two in the world) lasted only until the 11th green of his afternoon round with Woosnam. Again it wasn't that his opponent played badly on the day, rather that the Welshman played some wizard-like golf. In the morning he completed a round of 67, then after lunch

The referee steps in: Ian Woosnam has just thrashed José Maria Olazabal

reeled off a World Matchplay record of seven successive birdies from the 5th, after which Olazabal was forced to concede defeat, or as Michael Williams of the Daily Telegraph put it, 'Was on his knees and begging for mercy.'

In two days Ian Woosnam had played 59 holes and had scored an incredible 23 birdies plus one eagle. Who could possibly stop him now? The answer was Jeff Sluman in the semi-finals. And the reason was simply that Woosnam had drained the birdie well dry; the magical form had suddenly vanished and Sluman played a very measured game for a shock 3 and 2 victory. Meanwhile a titanic battle of the 'two Nicks' was taking place in the other semi-final. Price, who beat Faldo at the same stage the previous year, was two up at lunch but after a spell on the practice ground it was a different Faldo who emerged for the second 18 holes. He decided that he had been swinging too quickly in the morning, and now, slowing things down, was able to step up a gear and proceeded to play, in the words of his opponent, 'flawless golf' and at five under par for his afternoon round he emerged victorious 2 and 1.

Given their differing statures - in both senses of the word - the final was not surprisingly billed as 'David versus Goliath': would Faldo fold or would Sluman get slayed? This championship, remember, was all about form and fortunately for the Open champion his was not about to desert him now. What name is appropriate to describe a player who wins the first three holes in a

final, eagles the 12th, wins the last three holes of the morning round to go 6 up then finishes the match off with a birdie to win 8 and 7 - the biggest ever margin of victory in a Wentworth final? Goliath will do.

No white handkerchief, but Sluman (above) is about to surrender as Faldo (left) cruises to an 8 and 7 victory

1992 TOYOTA WORLD MATCHPLAY CHAMPIONSHIP

8 - 11 October, Wentworth (West Course), Surrey

FIRST ROUND
Jeff Sluman (USA) beat Vijay Singh (Fiji) 4 and 3
Ian Woosnam (Wales) beat Norio Suzuki (Japan) 8 and 6
Greg Norman (Aus) beat Brad Faxon (USA) 1 hole
Mark O'Meara (USA) beat Anders Forsbrand (Swe) at 37th
First round losers received £22,500

SECOND ROUND
Jeff Sluman beat Seve Ballesteros (Spain) 2 holes
Ian Woosnam beat José Maria Olazabal (Spain) 8 and 7
Nick Price (Zim) beat Greg Norman retired
Nick Faldo (England) beat Mark O'Meara 5 and 3
Second round losers received £27,500

SEMI FINALS
Jeff Sluman beat Ian Woosnam 4 and 3
Nick Faldo beat Nick Price 2 and 1

PLAY-OFF FOR 3RD AND 4TH PLACES
Nick Price beat Ian Woosnam 4 and 3
Price received £50,000; Woosnam £40,000

FINAL
Nick Faldo beat Jeff Sluman 8 and 7
Faldo received £160,000; Sluman £100,000

A second World Matchplay title for Faldo

THE WORLD MATCHPLAY
ROLL · OF · HONOUR

YEAR	WINNER				
1964	Arnold Palmer	1973	Gary Player	1983	Greg Norman
1965	Gary Player	1974	Hale Irwin	1984	Seve Ballesteros
1966	Gary Player	1975	Hale Irwin	1985	Seve Ballesteros
1967	Arnold Palmer	1976	David Graham	1986	Greg Norman
1968	Gary Player	1977	Graham Marsh	1987	Ian Woosnam
1969	Bob Charles	1978	Isao Aoki	1988	Sandy Lyle
1970	Jack Nicklaus	1979	Bill Rogers	1989	Nick Faldo
1971	Gary Player	1980	Greg Norman	1990	Ian Woosnam
1972	Tom Weiskopf	1981	Seve Ballesteros	1991	Seve Ballesteros
		1982	Seve Ballesteros	1992	Nick Faldo

1992 WPG EUROPEAN TOUR REVIEW

When myths become legends...

Should you ever have cause to visit the headquarters of the women's European Tour at Tytherington in Cheshire, do not be too shocked if you glimpse a large, mythical Arabian bird swooping overhead: it is a phoenix.

Just before the start of the 1992 season many commentators were predicting, if not the demise, certainly a sharp decline in the fortunes of the WPGE Tour. The logic driving this pessimistic view was that the Tour was caught up in a vicious circle from which there seemed no escape: a serious recession in Europe was causing sponsors and would-be sponsors to keep their money in their pockets; fewer sponsors meant fewer European tournaments; fewer tournaments meant many of the 'big names' would desert the Tour and play all their golf overseas - and no 'big names', no sponsors (with or without a recession). Yet in the space of just six months all pessimistic talk was crushed: like the mythical phoenix that rose from the ashes, the WPGE Tour experienced a sea change in its fortunes and, one assumes, its destiny.

Laura Davies won three times on the 1992 Tour and headed the Order of Merit

If the catalyst for the surge in confidence was Europe's astonishing victory in the Solheim Cup (reviewed separately ahead) the underlying reason why there is such cause for optimism (and the explanation for the triumph at Dalmahoy) is that the Tour has nurtured, and continues to nurture, a growing number of world class golfers - golfers who feel they owe more than a modicum of allegiance to their parent Tour.

England's Laura Davies is the role model: although she plays much of her golf in America, she still managed to play in all but two of the WPGE Tour's events, moreover, not only did she inspire her nine team mates to play the finest golf of their lives last October, but she enjoyed a brilliant season on her own account. 'Lion-hearted' Laura was one of two players who dominated in Europe; the other was Helen Alfredsson who, if she continues to improve as much over the next two years as she has done in the last, could well be the best woman golfer in the world by the end of 1994.

Davies captured three WPGE Tour events in 1992: she won the inaugural European Open by two shots in June; the English Open at Tytherington towards the end of July by seven (the biggest winning margin of the year and her 20th career victory) and the Italian Open by five strokes in September. The only event in which Laura failed to finish in the top 10 was the Weetabix British Open - ironically the Tour's biggest event. During one outstanding spell she played 14 consecutive rounds below par and concluded the season 75 under par for 34 rounds played. She finished as leading money winner and also collected the Vivien Saunders Award for recording the lowest stroke average (70.35). Quite some year!

Helen Alfredsson didn't compete in Europe as frequently as Davies (she was busy

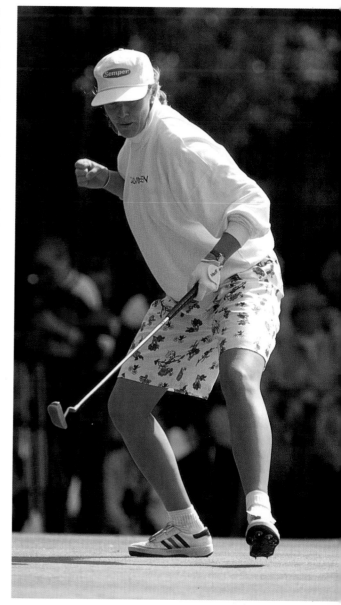

Helen Alfredsson on her way to a brilliant win in the Hennessy Ladies' Cup

securing the American LPGA Rookie of the Year prize ahead of Belgium's Florence Descampe) but looked a likely winner every time she did. Despite playing in only five Tour events she still managed to finish runner-up to Davies in the Order of Merit and came second in the scoring statistics with an average of 70.37. Significantly, in the five tournaments that both Davies and Alfredsson entered the Swede finished ahead of her rival on four occasions. In her five starts she had two wins, a 3rd, a 5th and a 6th place and was a total of 50 under par for 19 rounds played. Her European wins (she was also victorious in Japan late in the year) were at the Hennessy Ladies Cup in Cologne, one of the Tour's most sought after titles, where she produced a superb 67-66 finish to overhaul third round leader Trish Johnson (she birdied the 71st and 72nd holes) and the IBM Open in Stockholm following a close tussle with fellow Swede Lotte Neumann and Laura Davies. Alfredsson, like Davies, was undefeated in the Solheim Cup.

Notwithstanding the seers of doom, the season opened on a bright note with 21-year-old Stefania Croce, 'a petite Italian with a radiant smile', winning the Ford Classic at Woburn, leading from the start. The next three events were won by more established players: Alison Nicholas, Kitrina Douglas and Trish Johnson who respectively triumphed in the AGF Open, the BMW European Masters and the La Manga Classic.

Davies and Alfredsson now monopolised the winners rostrum for six tournaments, the one exception being French player Valerie Michaud's win in the Holiday Inn Leiden Open in Holland. Michaud is one of two outstanding French prospects, the other is Sandrine Mendiburu, and together they duelled season-long with Sweden's Carin Hjalmarsson (who scored an incredible 64 in the English Open) for the Rookie of the Year prize, which Mendiburu eventually won.

With the likes of Croce, Michaud and Mendiburu, plus the seemingly endless stream of talent emerging from Sweden, Europe's current Solheim Cup stars will not

be able to rest on their laurels - and if ever they do get too complacent they should be made to watch a video of Patty Sheehan's Weetabix British Open triumph at Woburn! The American, already the US Open champion, cruised to victory in that event setting a new course record 67 in the process. In fact only Australian Corinne Dibnah - leading moneywinner in 1991 - gave her a real run for her money (all

(Left) Kitrina Douglas won the BMW European Masters in 1992 and Sandrine Mendiburu (right) of France was the WPGE Tour's Rookie of the Year

£50,000 of it).

If the year started with a smile, courtesy of Croce, it ended on a stormy note. No, the pessimists hadn't resurfaced, just the weather. Rain interrupted the proceedings in the Slovenian Open staged at picturesque Bled (won by Karen Lunn), and typhoon Yvette reaped havoc at the 1st Sunrise Cup, the new women's equivalent of the World Cup of Golf, held in Taipei. But Yvette couldn't stop Neumann and Alfredsson from adding to Sweden's marvellous year - just as nothing it seems will be able to clip the wings of golf's swooping phoenix.

THE 1992 WEETABIX WOMEN'S BRITISH OPEN

24 - 27 September, Woburn G & CC

LEADING · SCORES

Patty Sheehan	68	72	67	207	£50,000
Corinne Dibnah	70	69	71	210	32,000
Marie Laure de Lorenzi	71	71	70	212	21,000
Liselotte Neumann	69	74	70	213	16,000
Patti Rizzo	72	70	72	214	11,600
Helen Alfredsson	74	72	68	214	11,600
Dottie Mochrie	74	68	73	215	9,000
Janice Arnold	70	74	72	216	6,120
Suzanne Strudwick	75	72	69	216	6,120
Florence Descampe	71	73	72	216	6,120
Malin Burstrom	72	73	71	216	6,120
Evelyn Orley	70	75	71	216	6,120
Karen Davies	75	70	73	218	4,560
Pamela Wright	73	76	69	218	4,560
Kristal Parker	72	74	72	218	4,560
Jane Geddes	78	69	72	219	4,300
Dale Reid	73	73	74	220	4,060
Alicia Dibos	75	75	70	220	4,060
Valerie Michaud	71	76	73	220	4,060
Tania Abitbol	72	71	78	221	3,550

Federica Dassu	73	77	71	221	3,550
Trish Johnson	73	73	75	221	3,550
Li Wen-Lin	74	70	77	221	3,550
Carin Hjalmarsson	74	75	72	221	3,550
Cindy Figg-Currier	71	77	73	221	3,550
Kathryn Marshall	74	73	74	221	3,550

Patty Sheehan (right and above) walks into the history books as the first player to achieve the US-British Open double

1992 WPG EUROPEAN TOUR SUMMARY

TOURNAMENT · WINNERS

Ford Ladies' Classic	Stefania Croce	(Italy)
AGF Ladies' Open de Paris	Alison Nicholas	(GB)
BMW European Masters	Kitrina Douglas	(GB)
Skol La Manga Club Classic	Trish Johnson	(GB)
The European Ladies' Open	Laura Davies	(GB)
Hennessy Ladies' Cup	Helen Alfredsson	(Swe)
Ladies' English Open	Laura Davies	(GB)
Holiday Inn Leiden Ladies' Open	Valerie Michaud	(Fra)
IBM Ladies' Open	Helen Alfredsson	(Swe)
BMW Italian Ladies' Open	Laura Davies	(GB)
Weetabix Women's British Open	Patty Sheehan	(USA)
Solheim Cup	Europe	
Slovenian Open	Karen Lunn	(Aus)
The Sunrise Cup - Women's World Team Championship	Sweden	

Stefania Croce was a popular winner of the Ford Classic

LEADING · MONEY · WINNERS

1	Laura Davies	£ 66,333
2	Helen Alfredsson	55,900
3	Corinne Dibnah	53,212
4	Trish Johnson	51,805
5	Catrin Nilsmark	35,728
6	Marie Laure de Lorenzi	34,922
7	Liselotte Neumann	34,202
8	Alison Nicholas	31,584
9	Kitrina Douglas	31,511
10	Sandrine Mendiburu	26,896
11	Alicia Dibos	26,509
12	Stefania Croce	24,329
13	Suzanne Strudwick	24,043
14	Dale Reid	20,081
15	Carin Hjalmarsson	20,015
16	Florence Descampe	19,425
17	Karen Lunn	18,636
18	Valerie Michaud	18,441
19	Allison Shapcott	17,879
20	Lisa Hackney	16,662
21	Janice Arnold	16,260
22	Kristal Parker	16,058
23	Lora Fairclough	15,770
24	Federica Dassu	14,493
25	Sofia Gronberg	13,606
26	Laurette Maritz-Atkins	13,210
27	Evelyn Orley	13,184
28	Corinne Soules	13,053
29	Jane Hill	12,656
30	Helen Wadsworth	12,606
31	Leigh Ann Mills	12,176
32	Gillian Stewart	11,906
33	Tania Abitbol	11,524
34	Debbie Dowling	11,519
35	Diane Barnard	11,368
36	Helen Dobson	11,171
37	Xonia Wunsch-Ruiz	11,098
38	Catherine Panton-Lewis	9,346
39	Kathryn Marshall	9,277
40	Sara Robinson	8,311
41	Li Wen-Lin	8,040
42	Malin Burstrom	7,890
43	Susan Moon	7,662
44	Kim Lasken	7,477
45	Karine Espinasse	7,443
46	Julie Forbes	7,436
47	Mardi Lunn	7,224
48	Regine Lautens	7,099
49	Claire Duffy	7,075
50	Nadene Hall	6,941

THE SOLHEIM CUP

THE 2ND SOLHEIM CUP

· ·

Proudly overlooked by an 18th century mansion and with Edinburgh Castle sitting on the horizon, the golf course at Dalmahoy is surrounded by history...

Where were you, at two minutes to two, on the 4th October 1992? That was the moment in history - a moment that will go down in history - when women's golf in Europe came of age. It was the instant when Catrin Nilsmark holed a two and a half foot putt to win her match against Meg Mallon and clinch the Solheim Cup for Europe. It was a victory that had looked a probability for an hour or so; had seemed a possibility for three days and had been a dream for two years.

In the inaugural match at Lake Nona in November 1990, it surprised no one when Europe's inexperienced golfers were beaten convincingly by a team of star-studded Americans. That the tables could be so

High Fives for two days became High Noon on Sunday

dramatically turned (from 11½-4½ in favour of the United States to 11½-6½ in favour of Europe) was a remarkable achievement, especially as several of the players on both sides at Dalmahoy had participated in that first encounter. A million difference reasons could be advanced as to why this incredible seesaw swing of fortune took place but ultimately there has to be only one principal reason: in just two years the Europeans had improved out of all recognition.

The American team comprised 10 players who between them had won 20 Major championships and 147 victories on the LPGA Tour. Facing them was a team with more talent than titles but with perhaps as much determination as any group of players in the history of international team golf. Winning the Solheim Cup meant as much to Mickey Walker's team as winning the Ryder

(Above) Dottie Mochrie couldn't stem the tide. (Left) Laura Davies was Europe's inspirational leader

Cup had to Tony Jacklin and Seve Ballesteros in the 1980s. It was heartening therefore, to say the least, that 17,000 people turned up in miserable weather to see them try.

Walker had determined her tactics for the first two days weeks before the event. In both the foursomes and fourball series she

led off with Laura Davies and Alison Nicholas. Davies was her most inspirational player - her Seve, you could say - and she and Nicholas had gelled well at Lake Nona in 1990. They gelled even better at Dalmahoy, for in the first foursomes match on the first day (Friday) they scored six birdies in the first 10 holes against the formidable pairing of Betsy King and Beth Daniel. The Americans made them fight all the way but the Europeans won one up and it provided an enormous tonic for the rest of the team. And they did exactly the same in the fourball matches on Saturday, shooting a better ball score of 66 for another one hole victory, this time over Patty Sheehan and Juli Inkster, who came first and second in the US Open.

The other pairings that Walker had decided upon were to link the Swedes, Helen Alfredsson and Lotte Neumann and the two Scots, Dale Reid and Pam Wright, and to play the fiery Belgian Florence Descampe with England's Trish Johnson.

Brilliantly following the Davies and Nicholas example, Europe gained a 4½-3½ lead after both the foursomes and fourball series had been completed. Neumann and Alfredsson were the other main source of the points, only failing to win both their matches when Pat Bradley, partnering Dottie Mochrie birdied the last for a half.

Over the first two days seven of the eight matches reached the 18th green and even the

one that didn't, made it to the 17th. So it was shaping up into a marvellously close contest with all to play for on the final day with its 10 singles matches.

Now, imagine how much confidence it inspires in a team to watch their star player fire two wood shots into the heart of a 495 yards par five opening hole (a hole which in the conditions no other player could get close to in two); to birdie that hole then pick up five further birdies before winning by 4 and 2? And how much more when your number two player is shaking hands with her opponent having won her match 4 and 3 at almost the same moment? Davies and Alfredsson did precisely that and it seemed to trigger an irresistible force that ran through the hearts of the of the home side.

The even match suddenly became uneven as the score boards began to tell an incredible story: Mickey Walker's Europeans were going to defeat the mighty Americans. At two minutes to two Nilsmark holed that winning putt and long before one minute to two she had been engulfed by her ecstatic team mates.

THE 2ND SOLHEIM CUP

2 - 4 October 1992, Dalmahoy G & CC, Lothian, Scotland

Heroines all:
captain Mickey
Walker and the
successful
European side
pose with the
magnificent
Waterford
crystal trophy

EUROPE	MATCHES	USA	MATCHES
FOURSOMES (FRIDAY)			
L. Davies & A. Nicholas (1 up)	1	B. King & B. Daniel	0
L. Neumann & H. Alfredsson (2 & 1)	1	P. Bradley & D. Mochrie	0
F. Descampe & T. Johnson	0	D. Ammaccapane & M. Mallon (1 up)	1
D. Reid & P. Wright	½	P. Sheehan & J. Inkster	½
FOURBALLS (SATURDAY)			
L. Davies & A. Nicholas (1 up)	1	P. Sheehan & J. Inkster	0
F. Descampe & T. Johnson	½	B. Burton & D. Richard	½
P. Wright & D. Reid	0	M. Mallon & B. King (1 up)	1
L. Neumann & H. Alfredsson	½	P. Bradley & D. Mochrie	½
SINGLES (SUNDAY)			
L. Davies (4 & 2)	1	B. Burton	0
H. Alfredsson (4 & 3)	1	D. Ammaccapane	0
T. Johnson (2 & 1)	1	P. Sheehan	0
A. Nicholas	0	J. Inkster (3 & 2)	1
F. Descampe	0	B. Daniel (2 & 1)	1
P. Wright (4 & 3)	1	P. Bradley	0
C. Nilsmark (3 & 2)	1	M. Mallon	0
K. Douglas	0	D. Richard (7 & 6)	1
L. Neumann (2 & 1)	1	B. King	0
D. Reid (3 & 2)	1	D. Mochrie	0
Europe 11½		**USA 6½**	

USA

1992 US PGA TOUR REVIEW

The search for new American superstars had become a romantic quest...

It is fair to say that 1992 will be a hard act to follow: just when it was beginning to look as if the US Tour might be losing some of its magic - its two most colourful characters, Greg Norman and Payne Stewart were struggling with niggling injuries and wretched form - along came Couples and Love. Together their names may sound like the recipe for a slush novel but the performances last year of Fred Couples and Davis Love, especially during a pulsating spring, were as refreshing as they were electrifying.

Their personalities and golf games are uncannily similar - modest and unassuming off the course; all grace and power on the

The Dream Team? Love and Couples dominated the American scene in 1992

course. If Couples deserves his bigger reputation, due in great part, of course, to the win at Augusta, he does so only just. Fred's run of form lasted longer (it is detailed in the report on the US Masters) but Davis enjoyed as many victories on the Tour in 1992, indeed more if one also includes his success late in the year in the Kapalua International, and the manner of his triumphs were just as impressive.

Players Championship at Sawgrass. Couples had the best round of the week, a brilliant 63, but it was Love who pulled away from a strong field to take the title by four shots from third round leader Nick Faldo, and from Tom Watson, Ian Baker-Finch and Phil Blackmar. He won two of his next three events as well, although the one that got away, unfortunately for Davis, but not Fred, was the Masters. Seven days after Couples

Ray Floyd – 50 years young

The 'Couples and Love Show' began in late February with Fred beating Davis in a play-off for the Los Angeles Open. Couples had already chalked up an astonishing nine-stroke victory in the Nestle Invitational before Love really moved into top gear. The week after the Nestle at Bay Hill was the occasion for the so called 'Fifth Major', the

was receiving his green jacket from Ian Woosnam, Love won the Heritage Classic for the third time in his career; once again his margin of victory was four. Then just a week after the success at Hilton Head came a dazzling six-shot win in the Greater Greensboro Open. This third win of the season was his most memorable, even if the

John Cook won three Tour events in 1992 and nearly won two Majors

April and throughout the year kept shooting absurdly low scores. He lost a play-off for the Byron Nelson Classic; he missed making the play-off in the Honda Classic by one and had a 63 in the Heritage Classic. (There was also a 64 in the first round of the Open Championship at Muirfield.) At the end of the year Floyd was playing much of his golf (and winning three times) on the Seniors Tour yet still found time to finish joint fifth in the Tour Championship at Pinehurst.

Family man Tom Kite, a mere stripling by comparison with Floyd at 42, won the Bellsouth Classic on Mothers Day and the US Open on Fathers Day. A second 42-year-old, Lanny Wadkins proved that he too can still produce the fireworks when required with a best of the day final round 65 which gave him victory in the Greater Hartford Open. It was Wadkins' 21st US Tour victory.

It will be interesting to see which (if any) of Floyd, Kite and Wadkins makes the US Ryder Cup team in 1993. One player who many expect to be on the plane bound for The Belfry in September is John Cook, arguably the surprise package of 1992. Although one's memories of Cook last year are dominated by his brave challenge for the Open at Muirfield and, to a lesser extent, his second place finish in the following Major, the USPGA at Bellerive, he did win three times in 1992 and finished the year third on the Money List behind Couples and Love with winnings in excess of $1 million. Two of Cook's wins came in 90-hole tournaments, the Bob Hope Chrysler Classic and the Las Vegas Invitational.

Players Championship was the more important, for he achieved it by turning a six-stroke deficit after 36 holes into a six-shot winning margin with an extraordinary final round 62. No other player in the field that day could score better than a 68 and Love's round included six birdies and two eagles. 'Just another incredible day in a month of great days' is how he cooly described his performance. Not a lot of slush there.

If there was a romantic or sentimental flavour to 1992 it wasn't provided by Love and Couples but by old timers Ray Floyd and Tom Kite. There is something extremely peculiar about Ray Floyd: the ageing process seems to have passed him by. There cannot be many professional golfers who are better at 50 than they were at 30 but he is one of them. Floyd won the prestigious Doral Ryder Open in March, nearly won the Masters in

Nobody will be more determined to play in the Ryder Cup than Mark Calcavecchia. Despite a number of second place finishes he hadn't won an event since his dramatic Open victory at Troon in 1989; 'hadn't', that is, until he charged to victory in the Phoenix

Open, scoring 69-65-67-63 to finish five ahead of the field. Calcavecchia played the last 29 holes in an incredible 15 under par. 'The Calc', as he is affectionately known, has become something of a streaky player, as evidenced by his scoring a first ever 29 on the back nine at Augusta (he birdied the last five holes of his final round) and a 63 in the World Series at Firestone (won by Craig Stadler) yet he never threatened to win either event.

Nine of America's winning team from Kiawah Island managed a win on the US Tour in 1992; in addition to the successes of Couples, Floyd, Wadkins and Calcavecchia there were wins for Corey Pavin, Steve Pate, Chip Beck, Mark O'Meara and Paul Azinger. Of these, Pavin's win in the Honda Classic was the most dramatic for he holed out with a full eight iron at the 72nd hole before going on to defeat Couples in a play-off;

(Left) Mark O'Meara should be given shares in Pebble Beach, and (below) Mark Calcavecchia's form is about as predictable as the English weather

Azinger's netted the most gold (and a highly significant title too, the Tour Championship at Pinehurst) but perhaps O'Meara's win was the most predictable as for the third time in four years he won the AT & T Pebble Beach Pro-Am. He also won the event in 1985 when it was known as 'The Bing Crosby'.

Couples, Love and Cook were the only triple winners on the PGA Tour in 1992, while four players achieved two wins: Brad Faxon, Canadian Richard Zokol, Nick Price and David Frost. In a year when not a single US Tour title was won by a European golfer, the first time that has happened since 1986, (Faldo came closest with his second place finishes in the Players Championship and the USPGA) Zimbabwean Price was the most successful overseas golfer. He finished fourth in the Money List, joining Couples, Love and Cook as one of the Tour's four 1992 millionaires, and of course captured his first Major title at Bellerive in August. Three other overseas players made it into the top 20 on the Money List: Steve Elkington, David Frost and Greg Norman.

South African Frost and Australian Elkington had very contrasting years: Frost missed the cut in seven of the first 12 tournaments he entered, yet suddenly rediscovered his form in late June to such an extent that he won the Buick Open by eight strokes, setting a new tournament record in the process! He later added the Hardee's Classic title, leading the event from start to finish. Elkington on the other hand played fairly consistently throughout the year; he won the opening event of 1992, the Tournament of Champions after a play-off with Brad Faxon but lost out in two other play-offs later in the year. Ample consolation for these two defeats however fell to Elkington with his success in the Heineken Australian Open in Sydney.

And so finally, what of our 'niggled' and 'wretched' duo from the opening paragraph, Messrs Stewart and Norman? Stewart, the 1991 US Open champion, will want to forget about 95% of 1992: he never really came close to winning a regular Tour event and finished a lowly 44th on the Money List, but he did at least 'hit the jackpot' - for the second year running in fact - in the annual year-end Skins Game. Nor was Greg Norman's year a vintage one by his standards. A knee operation sidelined Greg for most of the early part of the season and although he came very close to winning both the Freeport McMoran Classic and the Western Open (events won respectively by Chip Beck and Ben Crenshaw) and there were the occasional flashes of brilliance, such as a nine birdie 65 in the Colonial tournament, it wasn't until September's Canadian Open that he finally ended a two and half year winning drought.

Norman won that event in a way that only Norman could: his final round included an eagle two at the 6th, where he 'canned' a full five iron, and a final seven holes which comprised two bogeys, one double bogey and four birdies. Having been three ahead with five to play he needed to sink a 12-foot birdie putt at the last to tie Bruce Lietzke, which he duly did, then won the ensuing play-off with another birdie. Gary Van Sickle put it nicely when he wrote of Greg Norman in *Golf Illustrated* magazine, 'You're never quite sure if he's starring in Superman II, The Great Escape or Nightmare On Elm Street. Usually, it's a medley.'

If Payne Stewart can rediscover his winning ways and Greg Norman reproduces more of that Glen Abbey form in 1993 (with perhaps a good measure of his Johnnie Walker Jamaica form thrown in as well), it should be a great year to look forward to. Couples and Love can expect no honeymoon.

Australian Greg Norman with the Canadian Open trophy

1992 US PGA Tour Results

Australian Steve Elkington

January 9 - 12
Tournament of Champions
CARLSBAD, CALIFORNIA

* S Elkington	69	71	67	72	279	$144,000
B Faxon	68	70	71	70	279	86,400
F Couples	72	70	68	70	280	41,600
B Andrade	71	68	70	71	280	41,600
R Mediate	73	68	68	71	280	41,600
P Azinger	67	76	69	70	282	28,800
J D Blake	73	66	74	70	283	25,800
D Love III	69	71	73	70	283	25,800
M O'Meara	70	71	71	72	284	23,200
B McCallister	65	75	74	71	285	21,700

January 15 - 19
Bob Hope Chrysler Classic
BERMUDA DUNES, CALIFORNIA

* J Cook	65	73	63	69	66	336	$198,000
R Fehr	64	72	66	71	63	336	72,600
T Kite	65	73	68	67	63	336	72,600
G Sauers	69	65	64	70	68	336	72,600
M O'Meara	66	69	65	67	69	336	72,600
D Peoples	64	71	68	66	68	337	38,225
F Couples	68	67	69	64	69	337	38,225
T Lehman	70	65	70	67	66	338	30,800
D Love III	67	68	68	67	68	338	30,800
B Claar	71	63	67	68	69	338	30,800
K Perry	69	65	66	68	70	338	30,800

January 23-26
Phoenix Open
TPC SCOTTSDALE, ARIZONA

M Calcavecchia	69	65	67	63	264	$180,000
D Waldorf	68	67	67	67	269	108,000
R Mediate	69	66	69	67	271	68,000
J Huston	69	64	69	70	272	41,333
J Delsing	66	65	69	72	272	41,333
M O'Meara	70	68	65	69	272	41,333
E Fiori	72	63	70	68	273	29,100
G Hallberg	69	70	68	66	273	29,100
B Lietzke	73	67	67	66	273	29,100
B Lohr	68	68	67	70	273	29,100
N Price	66	68	71	68	273	29,100

January 29 - February 2
AT & T Pebble Beach National Pro-Am
PEBBLE BEACH, CALIFORNIA

* M O'Meara	69	68	68	70	275	$198,000
J Sluman	64	73	70	68	275	118,800
P Azinger	74	70	64	68	276	74,800
T Lehman	70	71	67	69	277	45,466
S Elkington	70	70	69	68	277	45,466
M Wiebe	64	74	70	69	277	45,466

L Rinker	72	66	72	69	279	35,475
G Morgan	71	69	69	70	279	35,475
T Watson	70	69	71	70	280	29,700
B Crenshaw	71	71	71	67	280	29,700
C Beck	67	71	73	69	280	29,700

B Lohr	72	65	66	203	30,250
J Mudd	68	69	66	203	30,250
D A Weibring	68	67	68	203	30,250
M Springer	66	65	72	203	30,250
T Watson	63	68	72	203	30,250

February 6 - 9
UNITED AIRLINES HAWAIIAN OPEN
WAIALAE, HONOLULU

J Cook	67	68	65	65	265	$216,000
P Azinger	65	67	68	67	267	129,600
J Maggert	68	68	67	68	271	81,600
W Levi	69	63	72	68	272	57,600
T Lehman	68	69	66	70	273	45,600
K Clearwater	68	70	66	69	273	45,600
J Woodward	67	71	70	66	274	40,200
L Mize	70	70	70	65	275	33,600
M Sullivan	69	67	69	70	275	33,600
M Brooks	69	71	65	70	275	33,600
J Gallagher Jnr	69	70	66	70	275	33,600

February 13 - 16
NORTHERN TELECOM OPEN
TPC AT STARPASS, TUCSON

L Janzen	71	67	67	65	270	$198,000
B Britton	67	70	68	66	271	118,800
D Toms	71	68	70	63	272	74,800
B Gardner	68	70	70	66	274	39,875
O Browne	70	68	70	66	274	39,875
J Gallagher Jnr	72	65	68	69	274	39,875
J D Blake	68	70	67	69	274	39,875
D Hart	69	69	65	71	274	39,875
K Green	71	65	68	70	274	39,875

February 20 - 23
BUICK INVITATIONAL
TORREY PINES, SAN DIEGO, CALIFORNIA

S Pate	64	69	67	200	$180,000
C Beck	70	65	66	201	108,000
S Elkington	65	68	69	202	52,000
R Wrenn	63	69	70	202	52,000
C Tucker	67	65	70	202	52,000
T Lehman	71	67	65	203	30,250

Fred Couples punches the air after winning the Los Angeles Open

February 27 - March 1
NISSAN LOS ANGELES OPEN
RIVIERA, CALIFORNIA

* F Couples	68	67	64	70	269	$180,000
D Love III	67	63	70	69	269	108,000
J Haas	67	69	69	65	270	58,000
Y Kaneko	69	69	67	65	270	58,000
R Mediate	67	68	66	70	271	40,000
S Lyle	67	67	66	72	272	40,000
D Martin	68	68	69	68	273	33,500
J Daly	68	70	70	66	274	28,000
S Elkington	70	70	68	66	274	28,000

* Winner in play-off

March 5 - 8
DORAL RYDER OPEN
DORAL RESORT & CC, MIAMI, FLORIDA

R Floyd	67	67	67	70	271	$252,000
K Clearwater	68	67	70	68	273	123,200
F Couples	66	69	69	69	273	123,200
K Green	69	70	68	67	274	61,600
D Love III	71	68	68	67	274	61,600
H Twitty	68	69	68	70	275	50,400
H Irwin	70	66	70	70	276	42,175
T Kite	73	68	66	69	276	42,175
M O'Meara	70	71	65	70	276	42,175
L Nelson	68	71	65	72	276	42,175
D Tewell	72	69	68	68	277	33,600
M Brooks	71	69	68	69	277	33,600

March 12 - 15
HONDA CLASSIC
WESTON HILLS, FORT LAUDERDALE, FLORIDA

* C Pavin	68	67	70	68	273	$198,000
F Couples	69	68	65	71	273	118,800
B R Brown	71	70	68	65	274	49,610
K Clearwater	66	70	70	68	274	49,610
R Floyd	66	68	71	69	274	49,610
B McCallister	68	68	68	70	274	49,610
M Brooks	69	70	64	71	274	49,610
B Lietzke	70	66	71	68	275	34,100
C Strange	72	70	68	66	276	30,800
A Magee	71	70	68	67	276	30,800

March 19 - 22
NESTLE INVITATIONAL
BAY HILL, ORLANDO, FLORIDA

F Couples	67	69	63	70	269	$180,000
G Sauers	70	70	65	73	278	108,000
M Brooks	68	75	69	69	281	45,100
J Huston	68	71	73	69	281	45,100
D Pohl	71	73	67	70	281	45,100
J Sluman	73	71	68	69	281	45,100
D Walfdorf	74	69	70	68	281	45,100
B Faxon	71	73	68	70	282	29,000
T Kite	76	69	67	70	282	29,000

D Love III	74	70	67	71	282	29,000
B Gardner	72	69	72	70	283	23,000
M Harwood	69	70	71	73	283	23,000
N Price	70	74	71	68	283	23,000

March 26 - 29
THE PLAYERS CHAMPIONSHIP
TPC AT SAWGRASS, PONTE VEDRA, FLORIDA

D Love III	67	68	71	67	273	$324,000
T Watson	68	70	70	69	277	118,800
I Baker-Finch	70	67	68	72	277	118,800
N Faldo	68	68	67	74	277	118,800
P Blackmar	67	69	68	73	277	118,800
T Sieckmann	71	72	67	68	278	62,550
C Parry	67	68	73	70	278	62,550
N Price	71	67	69	72	279	55,800
M O'Meara	69	69	74	68	280	46,800
J Mahaffey	71	71	69	69	280	46,800
J M Olazabal	69	65	75	71	280	46,800
M Brooks	67	70	70	73	280	46,800

April 2 - 5
FREEPORT McMORAN CLASSIC
ENGLISH TURN, NEW ORLEANS, LOUISIANA

C Beck	67	65	74	70	276	$180,000
G Norman	70	68	70	69	277	88,000
M Standly	69	73	66	69	277	88,000
B Bryant	67	69	71	72	279	44,000
J Maggert	68	69	67	75	279	44,000
N Faldo	74	69	69	69	281	30,250
N Lancaster	69	71	71	70	281	30,250
C Parry	72	68	71	70	281	30,250
J Inman	73	67	69	72	281	30,250
D Waldorf	68	71	70	72	281	30,250
L Rinker	70	69	69	73	281	30,250
S Ballesteros	67	73	73	69	282	22,000
T Kite	71	69	69	73	282	22,000

April 9 - 12
THE MASTERS
AUGUSTA NATIONAL, GEORGIA

(see p.37)

April 16 - 19
MCI HERITAGE CLASSIC
HARBOUR TOWN, HILTON HEAD, SOUTH CAROLINA

D Love III	67	67	67	68	269	$180,000
C Beck	69	65	71	68	273	108,000
N Price	71	71	66	66	274	68,000
R Cochran	70	69	70	66	275	44,000
F Zoeller	73	67	67	68	275	44,000
B Faxon	68	73	67	68	276	30,250
W Grady	69	70	70	67	276	30,250
W Levi	69	68	69	70	276	30,250
M O'Meara	69	65	70	72	276	30,250
K Perry	72	70	66	68	276	30,250
C Stadler	71	68	70	67	276	30,250

April 23 - 26
K-MART GREATER GREENSBORO OPEN
FOREST OAKS, GREENSBORO, TEXAS

D Love III	71	68	71	62	272	$225,000
J Cook	73	71	66	68	278	135,000
P Azinger	68	69	72	70	279	53,437
C Beck	69	67	75	68	279	53,437
T Byrum	71	67	70	71	279	53,437
T Kite	70	70	70	69	279	53,437
C Parry	73	69	68	69	279	53,437
M Reid	68	67	73	71	279	53,437
R Mediate	72	66	69	73	280	36,250
M Brooks	68	71	71	71	281	33,750

April 30 - May 3
SHELL HOUSTON OPEN
THE WOODLANDS, TEXAS

F Funk	68	72	62	70	272	$216,000
K Triplett	68	70	69	67	274	129,600
B R Brown	72	71	68	64	275	81,600
F Allem	67	70	66	73	276	57,600
M Brooks	71	67	67	72	277	45,600
B McCallister	69	69	69	70	277	45,600
R Fehr	70	69	68	71	278	36,150
D Forsman	69	69	73	67	278	36,150
R Gamez	70	67	77	64	278	36,150
N Price	72	67	69	70	278	36,150

Davis Love won three events in four weeks

May 7 - 10
BELLSOUTH CLASSIC
ATLANTA COUNTRY CLUB, MARIETTA, GEORGIA

T Kite	70	65	72	65	272	$180,000
J D Blake	69	68	70	68	275	108,000
R Cochran	73	66	71	69	279	58,000
L Mize	70	69	71	69	279	58,000
D Peoples	73	67	72	68	280	40,000
K Perry	72	71	68	70	281	34,750
P Burke	72	69	68	72	281	34,750
L Wadkins	72	74	69	67	282	31,000

May 14 - 17
GTE BYRON NELSON CLASSIC
TPC LAS COLINAS, IRVING, TEXAS

* B R Brown		69	64	66	199	$198,000
R Floyd		66	68	65	199	82,133
B Crenshaw		65	68	66	199	82,133
B Lietzke		65	67	67	199	82,133
J Woodward		69	68	63	200	40,150
M Dawson		70	63	67	200	40,150
J Haas		65	66	69	200	40,150

May 21 - 24
SOUTHWESTERN BELL COLONIAL
FORT WORTH, TEXAS

* B Lietzke	69	68	64	66	267	$234,000
C Pavin	68	64	70	65	267	140,400
J Gallagher Jnr	70	68	63	68	269	88,400
M Brooks	69	66	68	67	270	57,200
R Fehr	69	68	69	64	270	57,200
K Clearwater	66	69	69	68	272	42,087
J Cook	69	71	67	65	272	42,087
G Norman	70	68	69	65	272	42,087
D Pruitt	67	68	69	68	272	42,087

May 28 - 31
KEMPER OPEN
TPC AT AVENEL, MARYLAND

B Glasson	69	68	71	68	276	$198,000
J Daly	68	69	70	70	277	72,600
K Green	68	70	71	68	277	72,600
M Springer	70	68	71	68	277	72,600
H Twitty	71	70	69	67	277	72,600
M Brooks	71	70	70	67	278	34,430
M Calcavecchia	67	69	71	71	278	34,430
G Kraft	67	68	73	70	278	34,430
W Riley	71	67	73	67	278	34,430
P Stewart	70	68	70	70	278	34,430

June 4 - 7
THE MEMORIAL
MUIRFIELD VILLAGE, DUBLIN, OHIO

* D Edwards	71	65	70	67	273	$234,000
R Fehr	69	70	67	67	273	140,000
P Stewart	72	70	66	66	274	75,400
J Sindelar	69	65	67	73	274	75,400
N Henke	65	69	71	70	275	49,400
M Brooks	67	68	69	71	275	49,400
D Frost	72	70	69	65	276	37,830
L Mize	73	66	69	68	276	37,830
T Kite	74	67	67	68	276	37,830
V Singh	73	68	66	69	276	37,830
B Gilder	71	67	68	70	276	37,830

L Janzen	74	70	67	66	277	28,600
J Maggert	71	67	66	73	277	28,600
S Elkington	75	66	70	67	278	22,100
B Andrade	72	72	69	65	278	22,100
A Magee	71	67	71	69	278	22,100
T Purtzer	70	69	69	70	278	22,100
P Azinger	68	67	71	72	278	22,10 0

June 11 - 14
FEDERAL EXPRESS ST JUDE CLASSIC
TPC AT SOUTHWIND, MEMPHIS, TENESSEE

J Haas	68	67	64	64	263	$198,000
R Gamez	68	69	66	63	266	96,800
D Forsman	64	66	68	68	266	96,800
J McGovern	70	62	67	68	267	52,800
J Gallagher Jnr	69	65	66	68	268	44,000
H Twitty	68	70	66	65	269	35,612
N 'Joe' Ozaki	65	68	70	66	269	35,612
P Persons	63	70	69	67	269	35,612
S Gump	68	70	64	67	269	35,612

June 18 - 21
THE US OPEN CHAMPIONSHIP
PEBBLE BEACH, CALIFORNIA

(see page 49)

June 25 - 28
BUICK CLASSIC
WESTCHESTER CC, HARRISON, NEW YORK

D Frost	67	68	67	66	268	$180,000
D Waldorf	69	67	69	71	276	108,000
P Azinger	75	67	69	66	277	52,000
L Janzen	70	71	67	69	277	52,000
F Funk	69	67	71	70	277	52,000
C Parry	68	72	72	66	278	33,500
G Norman	71	73	65	69	278	33,500
T Kite	70	70	67	71	278	33,500
F Couples	71	67	72	69	279	25,000
C Stadler	72	67	71	69	279	25,000
M Smith	73	69	67	70	279	25,000
S Elkington	67	71	70	71	279	25,000
B Britton	71	67	69	72	279	25,000

July 2 - 5
CENTEL WESTERN OPEN
COG HILL, LAMONT, ILLINOIS

B Crenshaw	70	72	65	69	276	$198,000
G Norman	68	69	68	72	277	118,800
C Beck	70	71	70	67	278	52,800
B McCallister	64	73	71	70	278	52,800
D Waldorf	68	68	70	72	278	52,800
T Purtzer	73	69	68	69	279	35,475
J Sluman	72	72	63	72	279	35,475
R Cochran	71	72	69	68	280	25,457
B Fleisher	71	71	68	70	280	25,457
I Baker-Finch	65	72	74	69	280	25,457
B Claar	68	71	71	70	280	25,457
T Lehman	67	72	70	71	280	25,457
N Price	69	69	72	70	280	25,457
T Watson	70	69	70	71	280	25,457

July 9 - 12
ANHEUSER-BUSCH CLASSIC
KINGSMILL, VIRGINIA

D Peoples	66	69	67	69	271	$198,000
B Britton	68	71	64	69	272	82,133
E Dougherty	66	69	66	71	272	82,133
J Gallagher Jnr	69	67	68	68	272	82,133
T Lehman	67	68	71	67	273	44,000
J P Hayes	70	70	67	68	275	35,612
P H Horgan III	71	68	66	70	275	35,612
B Lietzke	72	63	68	72	275	35,612

July 16 - 19
CHATTANOOGA CLASSIC
COUNCIL FIRE, TENNESSEE

M Carnevale	68	71	66	64	269	$144,000
D Forsman	67	68	69	67	271	70,400
E Dougherty	69	69	62	71	271	70,400
S Lamontagne	66	72	69	66	273	33,067
B Fabel	69	66	70	68	273	33,067
D Edwards	66	71	67	69	273	33,067

Tom Kite plays from sand during the final round of the US Open at Pebble Beach

July 23 - 26
NEW ENGLAND CLASSIC
PLEASANT VALLEY, MASSACHUSETTS

B Faxon	66	67	67	68	268	$180,000
P Mickelson	66	69	69	66	270	108,000
G Sauers	69	70	66	66	271	48,000
S Elkington	66	68	69	68	271	48,000
D Peoples	70	66	67	68	271	48,000
J Cook	68	66	68	69	271	48,000
K Gibson	66	67	70	69	272	30,125
W Levi	66	68	68	70	272	30,125
L Hinkle	69	67	66	70	272	30,125
R Maltbie	65	66	69	72	272	30,125
M O'Meara	68	70	67	68	273	24,000
L Ten Broeck	67	67	68	71	273	24,000

July 30 - August 2
CANON GREATER HARTFORD OPEN
TPC AT RIVER HIGHLANDS, CROMWELL, CONNECTICUT

L Wadkins	68	70	71	65	274	$180,000
N Price	68	67	72	69	276	74,666
D Forsman	69	69	68	70	276	74,666
D Hammond	66	70	68	72	276	74,666
J Sluman	67	70	70	70	277	36,500
G Morgan	66	68	71	72	277	36,500
B Estes	68	69	68	72	277	36,500
P Blackmar	69	72	70	67	278	29,000
K Green	68	72	70	68	278	29,000
B Mayfair	69	66	71	72	278	29,000

August 6 - 9
BUICK OPEN
WARWICK HILLS, GRAND BLANC, MICHIGAN

* D Forsman	72	67	70	67	276	$180,000
S Elkington	70	69	67	70	276	88,000
B Faxon	69	69	70	68	276	88,000
R Freeman	74	69	66	68	277	44,000
J Huston	69	68	71	69	277	44,000
T Kite	72	69	72	65	278	34,750
G Lesher	68	71	71	68	278	34,750
D Rummells	71	68	70	70	279	30,000
M Sullivan	69	69	68	73	279	30,000

August 13 - 16
THE USPGA CHAMPIONSHIP
BELLERIVE, ST LOUIS, MISSOURI

(see page 75)

August 20 - 23
THE INTERNATIONAL
CASTLE PINES, COLORADO

	points	
Brad Faxon	14	$216,000
Lee Janzen	12	129,600
Steve Elkington	10	69,600
D A Weibring	10	69,600
John Daly	9	48,000
Greg Norman	8	40,200
Steve Pate	8	40,200
Bruce Lietzke	8	40,200
Keith Clearwater	7	34,800
Tom Watson	6	32,400
Joey Sindelar	5	30,000
Craig Stadler	4	27,600

August 27 - 30
NEC WORLD SERIES OF GOLF
FIRESTONE, AKRON, OHIO

C Stadler	69	65	69	70	273	$252,000
C Pavin	69	71	69	65	274	151,200
F Couples	67	70	70	68	275	95,200
J Cook	70	74	66	68	278	67,200
D Peoples	68	70	68	74	280	53,200
N Price	72	68	68	72	280	53,200
M Calcavecchia	73	71	63	74	281	45,150
A Magee	69	70	71	71	281	45,150
C Beck	65	70	77	70	282	39,200
D A Weibring	68	71	73	70	282	39,200
B Crenshaw	75	71	65	72	283	32,200
D Edwards	71	70	72	70	283	32,200
T Watson	70	70	73	70	283	32,200

There was no more popular win on the US Tour in 1992 than Ben Crenshaw's victory in the Western Open: he beat Greg Norman by a single stroke

September 3 - 6
GREATER MILWAUKEE OPEN
TUCKAWAY, WISCONSIN

R Zokol	67	71	64	67	269	$180,000
D Mast	67	69	71	64	271	108,000
T Lehman	68	67	72	66	273	52,000
D Hart	69	67	69	68	273	52,000
M Brooks	70	66	65	72	273	52,000
L Mize	70	67	69	68	274	33,500
P Stewart	68	72	67	67	274	33,500
N Price	69	71	65	69	274	33,500

September 10 -13
CANADIAN OPEN
GLEN ABBEY, OAKVILLE, ONTARIO

* G Norman	73	66	71	70	280	$180,000
B Lietzke	71	64	73	72	280	108,000
N Price	69	70	73	69	281	68,000
J Sindelar	70	74	71	67	282	41,333
J Delsing	71	71	71	69	282	41,333
C Pavin	67	74	71	70	282	41,333
K Clearwater	73	71	71	68	283	33,500
D Frost	71	70	73	70	284	28,000
M Wiebe	76	66	71	71	284	28,000
D Pooley	67	73	73	71	284	28,000
F Couples	71	69	71	73	284	28,000
J Daly	72	71	71	71	285	21,000
M O'Meara	72	73	68	72	285	21,000
F Quinn	68	72	72	73	285	21,000

September 17 - 20
HARDEE'S CLASSIC
OAKWOOD, COAL VALLEY, ILLINOIS

D Frost	62	68	64	72	266	$180,000
L Roberts	67	66	66	70	269	88,000
T Lehman	64	69	66	70	269	88,000
J Delsing	66	71	65	69	271	48,000
G Morgan	68	67	68	69	272	40,000
W Wood	64	72	71	66	273	32,375
J Sindelar	69	68	67	69	273	32,375
B Britton	69	70	65	69	273	32,375
P H Horgan III	67	68	67	71	273	32,375

September 24 - 27
BC OPEN
EN-JOIE, ENDICOTT, NEW YORK

J Daly	67	66	67	66	266	$144,000
J Edwards	69	66	69	68	272	52,000
K Green	65	69	69	69	272	52,000
N Henke	67	67	68	70	272	52,000
J Haas	69	68	67	68	272	52,000
K Clearwater	67	69	70	68	274	28,800
J Delsing	71	69	67	68	275	25,800
R Mediate	73	65	71	66	275	25,800
J Sindelar	71	69	70	66	276	22,400
M Hulbert	70	72	70	64	276	22,400

October 1 - 4
BUICK SOUTHERN OPEN
CALLAWAY GARDENS, GEORGIA

G Hallberg	68	69	69	206	$126,000
J Gallagher Jnr	69	68	70	207	75,600
L Roberts	71	70	68	209	47,600
G Sauers	71	71	68	210	27,563
L Silveira	71	70	69	210	27,563
P Mickelson	68	75	68	211	20,300
J Daly	67	71	73	211	20,300

October 8 - 11
LAS VEGAS INVITATIONAL
TPC AT SUMMERLIN, LAS VEGAS, NEVADA

* J Cook	68	66	62	70	68	334	$234,000
D Frost	71	67	67	68	63	336	140,400
E Estes	68	70	65	68	67	338	62,400
D Love III	70	66	71	64	67	338	62,400
N Henke	68	68	71	63	68	338	62,400
J Adams	66	67	68	68	69	338	62,400
R Gamez	68	64	70	68	69	339	43,550
M Standly	66	71	65	72	66	340	37,700
P Azinger	66	69	68	68	69	340	37,700
K Clearwater	70	66	66	68	70	340	37,700

October 15 - 18
WALT DISNEY WORLD OLDSMOBILE CLASSIC
LAKE BUENA VISTA, FLORIDA

J Huston	66	68	66	62	262	$180,000
M O'Meara	64	68	64	69	265	108,000
T Schulz	66	66	64	71	267	68,000
P Stewart	64	67	67	70	268	48,000
D Waldorf	65	68	67	69	269	40,000
B Britton	67	65	68	70	270	34,750
L Janzen	62	70	68	70	270	34,750
D Edwards	72	64	68	67	271	29,000
L Roberts	69	65	69	68	271	29,000
R Mediate	69	65	67	70	271	29,000

October 22 - 25
HEB TEXAS OPEN
OAK HILLS, SAN ANTONIO, TEXAS

* N Price	67	62	68	66	263	$162,000
S Elkington	68	65	65	65	263	97,200
D Edwards	66	68	68	65	267	46,800
C Pavin	63	69	67	68	267	46,800
J Maggert	67	65	67	68	267	46,800

D Hammond	69	63	67	69	268	32,400
P Stewart	68	66	72	63	269	24,364
B Bryant	67	65	71	66	269	24,364
M Hatalsky	71	66	66	66	269	24,364
L Janzen	68	65	69	67	269	24,364
M Brooks	66	67	68	68	269	24,364

October 29 - November 1
TOUR CHAMPIONSHIP
PINEHURST, NORTH CAROLINA

P Azinger	70	66	69	71	276	$360,000
L Janzen	74	68	69	68	279	177,000
C Pavin	74	68	69	68	279	177,000
K Clearwater	68	75	72	67	282	96,000
F Couples	73	78	66	66	283	76,000
R Floyd	72	71	71	69	283	76,000
B Faxon	70	71	72	71	284	59,000
D Forsman	71	67	72	74	284	59,000
D Frost	69	68	74	73	284	59,000
J Haas	72	66	73	73	284	59,000
G Norman	70	70	73	71	284	59,000
D Waldorf	70	73	70	71	284	59,000

* Winner in play-off

Paul Azinger won the Tour's richest event last year: a Major championship success is now long overdue

1992 US PGA TOUR

TOURNAMENT · WINNERS

January

TOURNAMENT OF CHAMPIONS	Steve Elkington*	(Aus)
BOB HOPE CHRYSLER CLASSIC	John Cook*	(US)
PHOENIX OPEN	Mark Calcavecchia	(US)
AT&T PEBBLE BEACH PRO-AM	Mark O'Meara*	(US)

February

UA HAWAIIAN OPEN	John Cook	(US)
NORTHERN TELECOM OPEN	Lee Janzen	(US)
BUICK INVITATIONAL	Steve Pate	(US)
NISSAN LOS ANGELES OPEN	Fred Couples*	(US)

March

DORAL RYDER OPEN	Ray Floyd	(US)
HONDA CLASSIC	Corey Pavin*	(US)
NESTLE INVITATIONAL	Fred Couples	(US)
PLAYERS CHAMPIONSHIP	Davis Love III	(US)

April

FREEPORT-McMORAN CLASSIC	Chip Beck	(US)
THE MASTERS	Fred Couples	(US)
DEPOSIT GUARANTY CLASSIC	Richard Zokol	(Can)
MCI HERITAGE CLASSIC	Davis Love III	(US)
GREATER GREENSBORO OPEN	Davis Love III	(US)
SHELL HOUSTON OPEN	Fred Funk	(US)

May

BELLSOUTH CLASSIC	Tom Kite	(US)
BYRON NELSON CLASSIC	Billy Ray Brown*	(US)
SOUTHWESTERN BELL COLONIAL	Bruce Lietzke*	(US)
KEMPER OPEN	Bill Glasson	(US)

June

MEMORIAL TOURNAMENT	David Edwards*	(US)
FEDERAL EXPRESS ST JUDE CLASSIC	Jay Haas	(US)
US OPEN	Tom Kite	(US)
BUICK CLASSIC	David Frost	(S Afr)

July

CENTEL WESTERN OPEN	Ben Crenshaw	(US)
ANHEUSER-BUSCH CLASSIC	David Peoples	(US)
CHATTANOOGA CLASSIC	Mark Carnevale	(US)
NEW ENGLAND CLASSIC	Brad Faxon	(US)
CANON GREATER HARTFORD OPEN	Lanny Wadkins	(US)

August

BUICK OPEN	Dan Forsman*	(US)
USPGA CHAMPIONSHIP	Nick Price	(Zim)
THE INTERNATIONAL	Brad Faxon	(US)
NEC WORLD SERIES OF GOLF	Craig Stadler	(US)

September

GREATER MILWAUKEE OPEN	Richard Zokol	(Can)
CANADIAN OPEN	Greg Norman*	(Aus)
HARDEE'S GOLF CLASSIC	David Frost	(S Afr)
BC OPEN	John Daly	(US)

October

BUICK SOUTHERN OPEN	Gary Hallberg	(US)
LAS VEGAS INVITATIONAL	John Cook	(US)
WALT DISNEY CLASSIC	John Huston	(US)
HEB TEXAS OPEN	Nick Price*	(Zim)
TOUR CHAMPIONSHIP	Paul Azinger	(US)

* Winner in play-off

1992 US PGA TOUR

LEADING · MONEY · WINNERS

1	Fred Couples	$ 1,344,188	34	Fred Funk	416,930	68	Bruce Fleisher	236,516
2	Davis Love III	1,191,630	35	Joey Sindelar	395,354	69	Brad Bryant	227,529
3	John Cook	1,165,606	36	Bill Britton	391,700	70	Mark Carnevale	220,922
4	Nick Price	1,135,773	37	John Daly	387,455	71	Brad Fabel	220,495
5	Corey Pavin	980,934	38	Jeff Maggert	377,408	72	Robert Gamez	215,648
6	Tom Kite	957,445	39	Mark Calcavecchia	377,234	73	Mike Standly	213,712
7	Paul Azinger	929,863	40	Lanny Wadkins	366,837	74	Fulton Allem	209,982
8	Brad Faxon	812,093	41	Ken Green	360,397	75	Peter Persons	203,625
9	Lee Janzen	795,279	42	Nick Faldo	345,168	76	Billy Andrade	202,509
10	Dan Forsman	763,109	43	Loren Roberts	338,673	77	Donnie Hammond	197,085
11	Mark O'Meara	759,648	44	Payne Stewart	334,738	78	Brian Claar	192,255
12	Steve Elkington	746,352	45	Nolan Henke	326,387	79	Billy Mayfair	191,878
13	Ray Floyd	741,918	46	Russ Cochran	326,290	80	Bob Estes	190,778
14	Jeff Sluman	729,027	47	Larry Mize	316,428	81	Kenny Perry	190,455
15	David Frost	717,883	48	Richard Zokol	311,909	82	Dillard Pruitt	189,604
16	Bruce Lietzke	703,805	49	Rocco Mediate	301,896	83	Wayne Grady	183,361
17	Chip Beck	689,704	50	Tom Watson	299,818	84	Mike Smith	178,964
18	Greg Norman	676,443	51	Jay Don Blake	299,298	85	Kirk Triplett	175,868
19	Jim Gallagher Jnr	638,314	52	Jay Delsing	296,740	86	Mark Wiebe	174,763
20	Jay Haas	632,628	53	Andrew Magee	285,946	87	John Inman	173,828
21	Mark Brooks	629,754	54	Bill Glasson	283,765	88	Tom Sieckmann	173,424
22	Keith Clearwater	609,273	55	Mike Hulbert	279,577	89	John Adams	173,069
23	Duffy Waldorf	582,120	56	Gil Morgan	272,959	90	Phil Mickelson	171,714
24	Tom Lehman	579,093	57	Howard Twitty	264,042	91	Bob Gilder	170,761
25	David Peoples	539,531	58	Ian Baker-Finch	262,817	92	Jim McGovern	169,888
26	John Huston	515,453	59	Blaine McCallister	261,187	93	Tom Purtzer	166,722
27	David Edwards	515,070	60	Ted Schulz	259,204	94	Larry Rinker	163,954
28	Craig Stadler	487,460	61	Dudley Hart	254,903	95	Jim Woodward	161,301
29	Billy Ray Brown	485,151	62	D A Weibring	253,018	96	Doug Tewell	159,856
30	Steve Pate	472,626	63	Phil Blackmar	242,783	97	Scott Simpson	155,284
31	Ben Crenshaw	439,071	64	Craig Parry	241,901	98	Dick Mast	150,847
32	Gene Sauers	434,566	65	Wayne Levi	237,935	99	Curtis Strange	150,639
33	Rick Fehr	433,003	66	Ed Dougherty	237,525	100	Ed Humenik	149,337
			67	Gary Hallberg	236,629			

1992 LPGA Tour Review

• •

It was the year when Dottie made a Mochrie of the form book...

An even numbered year perhaps, but 1992 was an odd year on the LPGA Tour. Very odd. In 1990 Beth Daniel was the leading money winner, notching up seven tournament victories then adding two more titles the following year; Pat Bradley won three events in 1990 and led the Order of Merit in 1991, collecting four wins and entering the Hall of Fame en route, and then there was Meg Mallon, the double Major winner of 1991 and runner-up to Bradley in the money stakes. Hard to believe then that Daniel, Bradley and Mallon couldn't muster a single victory between them on the 1992 LPGA Tour. Imagine Faldo, Woosnam and Olazabal all failing in the same season. Such a scenario would normally suggest an uneventful year but this was far from the case on the 1992 LPGA Tour: exciting new stars emerged and several players produced dazzling bursts of form; in fact 1992 was the year of the purple patch.

Chiefly responsible for making a mockery of the 1990 and 1991 form book was Mochrie: Dottie Mochrie who trebled her total of LPGA career victories by winning four times. In fact Mochrie was the only player whose purple patch continued season long. The win that paved the way for a tumultuous year was a play-off success against Juli Inkster in the first LPGA Major of

1992, April's Nabisco Dinah Shore. Two weeks later she won the Sega Championship and later triumphed in the Welch's Classic and the Sun-Times Challenge. Mochrie easily topped the LPGA Order of Merit with winnings of $693,335; she also received the LPGA Player of the Year Award and for good measure teamed up win Dan Forsman in the first week of December to win the JC Penny (Mixed Team) Classic in Florida.

During the JC Penny Classic Forsman was widely quoted as saying that his partner reminded him of 'a young Tom Watson' who once possessed 'the same kind of unabashed confidence.'

If there is a woman golfer with even greater memories to cherish of 1992 than Dottie Mochrie then it is Patty Sheehan. Her form was by no means as consistent as Mochrie's last year but she had easily the most celebrated and significant purple patch. In a space of five weeks she won three tournaments, culminating in the biggest prize of all, the US Women's Open at Oakmont. If ever a famous course produced a worthy champion it was Oakmont in 1992, when Sheehan at last won a title that she and her supporters must have begun to think was never destined to grace her cabinet. (It was Sheehan, you may recall, who once frittered away a nine stroke lead on the final day of the championship.) Sheehan only just won at

1992 LPGA Player of the Year, Dottie Mochrie has been tipped to become the Tom Watson of women's golf

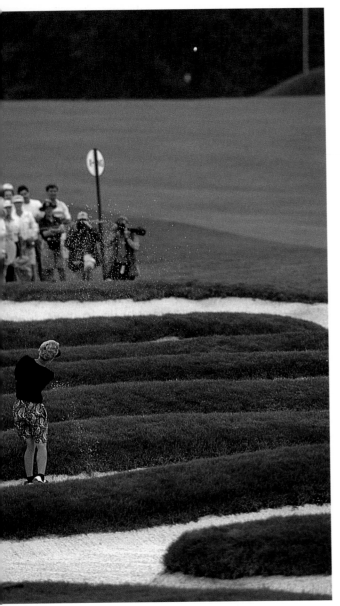

The famous 'church pew' bunkers at Oakmont

by winning the Weetabix Women's British Open at Woburn, the 'fifth Major championship' of the women's game.

During the early part of the season the two players challenging Mochrie for supremacy on the Tour were two of its rising stars, big-hitting Brandie Burton and Danielle Ammaccapane, and towards the end of the year the major talking point was the brilliant return to form of Nancy Lopez. Perhaps the most popular woman golfer of all time, Lopez won successive tournaments in September and finished the season in 8th place on the Order of Merit. The famous smile was back.

If the overdue successes of Mochrie and Sheehan in the Nabisco and US Open championships were non too amazing the victories of Betsy King and Sherri Steinhauer in the LPGA's other two Majors were. King, a double US Open champion winning a Major amazing? It wasn't so much the fact that she won the Mazda LPGA Championship (although her form earlier in the season had been fairly poor) but the majestic manner of her victory. King destroyed the field at Bethesda in May, winning by 11 strokes with rounds of 68-66-67-66. She smashed numerous scoring records, including becoming the first player in LPGA history to break 70 in all four rounds of a Major championship. King summed up her astonishing performance when she said, 'These were the best four days of golf I've ever played.' Not surprisingly King used her victory as the platform for another successful season with two further wins and she finished the year ahead of everyone on the Order of Merit table except Mochrie.

Sherri Steinhauer's win in the du Maurier Classic in Winnipeg was quite an upset simply because, good player that everyone knew she was, it was her maiden LPGA

Oakmont though, beating the luckless Juli Inkster in a second Major play-off after brilliantly birdieing the 71st and 72nd holes to tie her close friend. There were no more wins for Sheehan on the LPGA Tour but later in the year she crossed the Atlantic and completed a unique US-British Open double victory. Not many doubt that Steinhauer will win again soon.

With players of the calibre of Sheehan, King and Mochrie it is still hard to believe that the United States were beaten so convincingly by Europe in the Solheim Cup. The indifferent form of players like Bradley and Daniel only provides a partial explanation.

The biggest factor however, was surely the emergence, or arrival, of a number of outstanding European players, who in addition to their exploits in Europe on the WPGE Tour, made a significant impression on the LPGA Tour in 1992. Laura Davies and Lotte Neumann - both still in their 20s - were already well known, indeed both have a US Open win to their credit, but the high-class performances of Sweden's Helen Alfredsson and Belgium's Florence Descampe took most LPGA observers by surprise. With a little more experience Alfredsson could easily have won three tournaments: on two occasions she was leading with two holes to play before over-eagerness caused her to make costly mistakes. Descampe didn't play

Statuesque or static? Belgian Florence Descampe

Betsy King enjoyed the finest win of the year

as consistently well as Alfredsson but she did beat her Solheim Cup team mate to a first LPGA success, winning the McCall's Classic at Stratton Mountain two weeks after the US Open. Adequate consolation came for Alfredsson however in the form of the LPGA's Rookie of the Year Award. The bad news for Mochrie and Co. is that Descampe and Alfredsson are ever improving while Laura Davies appears to have recaptured her best form. And if that weren't enough there will be even more Europeans playing on the LPGA Tour in 1993, all fired up with post Dalmahoy-induced delirium.

THE 1992 LPGA MAJORS

27 - 29 March
NABISCO DINAH SHORE
MISSION HILLS, PALM SPRINGS

* D Mochrie	69	71	70	69	279	$105,000
J Inkster	72	68	68	71	279	65,165
* (Mochrie won at first playoff hole)						
B Burton	70	72	71	68	281	42,269
P Sheehan	71	69	69	72	281	42,269
M Mallon	73	69	72	68	282	29,940
S Steinhauer	72	73	69	70	284	22,719
D Eggeling	67	78	69	70	284	22,719
K Tschetter	73	71	73	68	285	15,778
P Wright	74	71	71	69	285	15,778
B Daniel	70	68	76	71	285	15,778
M McGann	68	74	71	72	285	15,77 8

14 - 17 May
MAZDA LPGA CHAMPIONSHIP
BETHESDA, MARYLAND

B King	68	66	67	66	267	$150,000
K Noble	73	70	70	65	278	71,287
L Neumann	71	68	70	69	278	71,287
J Carner	71	66	70	71	278	71,287
D Mochrie	71	73	68	67	279	38,998
H Alfredsson	69	69	68	73	279	38,998
P Sheehan	71	70	69	70	280	27,928
A Ritzman	68	71	71	70	280	27,928
J Inkster	70	71	66	74	281	23,651
B Burton	68	73	70	71	282	20,128
A Alcott	69	69	73	71	282	20,128

23 - 26 July
47TH US WOMEN'S OPEN
OAKMONT, PENNSYLVANIA

* P Sheehan	69	72	70	69	280	$130,000
J Inkster	72	68	71	69	280	65,000
* (Sheehan won 18-hole playoff, 72 to 74)						
D Andrews	69	73	72	70	284	38,830
M Mallon	73	72	72	70	287	28,336

D Coe	71	71	72	74	288	22,295
G Graham	72	71	71	75	289	17,472
D Mochrie	70	74	72	73	289	17,472
M McGann	72	73	70	74	289	17,472
T Green	72	75	70	73	290	13,372
J Geddes	73	70	78	70	291	13,372
P Wright	70	69	76	76	291	13,372
M Edge	73	74	72	73	292	11,731
A Alcott	76	74	73	70	293	10,887
H Alfredsson	71	79	72	71	293	10,887
L Neumann	76	72	72	74	294	10,111
N Lopez	75	76	71	73	295	8,674
S Strudwick	75	73	73	74	295	8,674
O-H Ku	73	74	74	74	295	8,674
B King	74	73	73	75	295	8,674

13 - 16 August
DU MAURIER CLASSIC
ST CHARLES CC, WINNIPEG, CANADA

S Steinhauer	67	73	67	70	277	$105,000
J Dickinson	70	71	67	71	279	65,165
J Inkster	70	69	73	68	280	47,553
E Gibson	71	73	74	65	283	36,985
S Hamlin	74	68	75	67	284	29,940
T Barrett	74	71	70	70	285	17,269
D Andrews	73	69	72	71	285	17,269
B Mucha	71	71	72	71	285	17,269
F Descampe	71	71	70	73	285	17,269

Patty Sheehan
and Juli Inkster
at the US
Women's Open

THE 1992 LPGA TOUR

TOURNAMENT · WINNERS

Oldsmobile LPGA Classic	C. Walker	Shoprite LPGA Classic	A. M. Palli
Phar-Mor At Inverrary	S. Hamlin	Lady Keystone Open	D. Ammaccapane
Itoki Hawaiian Open	L. Walters	Rochester International	P. Sheehan
Kemper Open	D. Coe	Jamie Farr Toledo Classic	P. Sheehan
Inamori Classic	J. Dickinson	The Phar-Mor In Youngstown	B. King
Ping/Welch's Championship	B. Burton	JAL Big Apple Classic	J. Inkster
Standard Register Ping	D. Ammaccapane	U.S. Women's Open Championship	
Nabisco Dinah Shore	D. Mochrie		P. Sheehan
Las Vegas International	D. Lofland	Welch's Classic	D. Mochrie
Sega Championship	D. Mochrie	McCall's LPGA Classic at	
Sara Lee Classic	M. Will	Stratton Mountain	F. Descampe
Centel Classic	D. Ammaccapane	Du Maurier Ltd Classic	S. Steinhauer
Crestar-Farm Fresh Classic	J. Wyatt	Northgate Computer Classic	K. Tschetter
Mazda LPGA Championship	B. King	Sun-Times Challenge	D. Mochrie
LPGA Corning Classic	C. Walker	Rail Charity Golf Classic	N. Lopez
McDonald's Championship	A. Okamoto	Ping-Cellular One Championship	N. Lopez
Oldsmobile Classic	B. Mucha	Safeco Classic	C. Walker

LEADING · MONEY · WINNERS

1	Dottie Mochrie	$693,335	18	Michelle McGann	239,062	34	Shelley Hamlin	157,327
2	Betsy King	551,320	19	Pat Bradley	238,541	35	Jane Crafter	155,485
3	Danielle Ammaccapane	513,639	20	Ayako Okamoto	229,953	36	Cindy Rarick	155,303
4	Brandie Burton	419,571	21	Liselotte Neumann	225,667	37	Tammie Green	154,717
5	Patty Sheehan	418,622	22	Missie Berteotti	213,720	38	Anne Marie Palli	153,065
6	Meg Mallon	400,052	23	Nancy Scranton	213,225	39	Laura Davies	150,163
7	Juli Inkster	392,063	24	Florence Descampe	210,281	40	Amy Benz	141,673
8	Nancy Lopez	382,128	25	Rosie Jones	204,096	41	Dale Eggeling	138,781
9	Colleen Walker	368,600	26	Alice Ritzman	201,922	42	Jan Stephenson	132,634
10	Judy Dickinson	351,559	27	Barb Mucha	190,519	43	Michelle Estill	132,399
11	Beth Daniel	329,681	28	Tina Barrett	184,719	44	Hollis Stacy	132,323
12	Sherri Steinhauer	315,145	29	JoAnne Carner	175,880	45	Marta Figueras-Dotti	127,789
13	Donna Andrews	299,839	30	Kristi Albers	173,189	46	Maggie Will	126,428
14	Dana Lofland	270,413	31	Caroline Keggi	172,669	47	Mitzi Edge	117,835
15	Deb Richard	266,427	32	Jane Geddes	164,127	48	Pamela Wright	116,775
16	Helen Alfredsson	262,115	33	Kris Tschetter	157,436	49	Karen Noble	110,278
17	Dawn Coe	251,392				50	Elaine Crosby	109,125

AUSTRALIA

1992 AUSTRALASIAN TOUR REVIEW

·······························

**One can occasionally Parry a Shark in February
but how does one resist an Elk in November?...**

The Australasian Tour teed off in January with 40-year-old Rodger Davis winning an event on the Gold Coast, just south of Brisbane, and it holed out in December with 41-year-old Rodger Davis winning an event on the Sunshine Coast, just north of Brisbane. A nice bit of symmetry it appears until you note the fact that Davis won the former at the opulent resort of Sanctuary Cove with a final round 77 and the latter, at the equally opulent resort of Coolum, with a closing 65. Twelve shots and twelve months the difference - and an awful lot happened in between.

When the Tour wasn't rowing with its European counterpart over whether or not it was fair game (or fair dinkum) for the Volvo Tour to stage events in the Pacific Rim countries (the Royal and Ancient game's mini Cuban Crisis), some marvellous golf was

Plane? What plane? Peter Senior seems unperturbed by low-flying aircraft

First and last: Rodger Davis won twice in 1992; once in January and again in December

being played at some marvellous courses. While Rodger had to wait almost a year for his next victory, Queensland golf fans only had to wait seven days before they witnessed a tournament-winning 65. It was at the Palm Meadows Cup, just down the road from Sanctuary Cove and Ireland's Ronan Rafferty charged through a distinguished field firing six birdies and an eagle in the space of 10 holes on the final day. The famous palms probably shook in disbelief.

From Palms to Vines and yet another sumptuous resort, this time on the other side of Australia. The third event on the 1992 Tour produced a welcome win for Ian Baker-Finch, then the reigning British Open champion, his first success after his storming win at Royal Birkdale. Baker-Finch made heavier weather of winning the Vines Classic near Perth, but one suspects that the renowned wine buff might have been a little distracted by the wafting bouquets from the many magnificent nearby vineyards.

After three events staged over spectacular modern resort layouts it was time for a touch of the traditional: and in Australia they don't come more traditional than the famous sand-belt courses of greater Melbourne.

Two of the best in the area, Kingston Heath and Huntingdale hosted the Australian Matchplay and the Australian Masters events in February. Mike Clayton won the Matchplay defeating fellow Aussie Peter McWhinney, who later in the year finished joint second in the Heineken Australian Open, and Craig Parry won the Masters after Greg Norman bogeyed three of his last four holes (as he had done in 1991) to miss out on a seventh Gold Jacket. 'Greg blows another big one' blasted the headlines, but then it is a million times more easy to make critical comments than to achieve successive finishes of first, first, second, second in one of the world's premier tournaments.

Craig Parry, the Ian Woosnam of Australian golf, won again two weeks later, grabbing the New South Wales Open after a play-off with Ken Trimble and one of those brilliant final round 65s. Sandwiching Parry's two victories was Kiwi Grant Waite's success in the New Zealand Open which was played at yet another celebrated golf course - probably the finest in New Zealand - the Paraparaumu course near Wellington.

The Australasian Tour went into hibernation after the New South Wales Open, not reappearing until mid-October when it surfaced in Malaysia. Perhaps the player who had been looking forward most eagerly for that resumption was Robert Allenby. We haven't mentioned him until now for he hadn't come especially close to winning an event in what was his Rookie year; the high level and consistency of his performances however was already suggesting that here was a player of great promise. Twenty-year-old Allenby had turned professional at the end of the 1991 season after finishing a superb second to Wayne Riley in the Australian Open at Royal Melbourne. In his first professional event he missed the cut at Sanctuary Cove but

bounced back immediately with a fourth place at Palm Meadows. He then came fifth in the Vines Classic; made the semi-final of the Australian Matchplay; was joint fourth at Huntingdale and third in the NSW Open. Not too many were surprised then when he gained his first professional victory in the Perak Masters in Malaysia, the first tournament of the second half of the Australasian circuit.

The following two events were staged in Singapore and Malaysia again, and then the Tour paid New Zealand a second visit for the Air New Zealand/Shell Open. For much of the four days it looked as if one of New Zealand's two Maori amateur prodigies, Phil Tataurangi or Michael Campbell, who helped win the Eisenhower Trophy for New Zealand, might pull off an amazing victory; eventually however the player most had turned up to watch, the recently crowned USPGA Champion Nick Price, stole the show with a fantastic 63 in the final round.

Royal Adelaide was the Tour's next port of call. Like Royal Melbourne, Royal Adelaide is a real golfing masterpiece designed by

Taking a breather – Colin Montgomerie looks shattered after a long season

Alister Mackenzie. Last November Brett Ogle retained his South Australian Open title there by virtue of timely birdies at the 70th and 71st holes. The previous week Ogle had captured the individual prize in the World Cup of Golf at La Moraleja in Spain and his double success prompted Peter Thomson to declare, 'There's no finer player in Australia when he's on form.' Mind you, he said much the same thing of Craig Parry a week later

Open (won by Steve Elkington and reviewed ahead), and so no golfer, Greg Norman included, has yet been able to win Australia's Masters, Open and PGA titles in the same year - the 'Australian Grand Slam'. In fact, Parry missed the cut at The Lakes. One man who didn't make an exit after 36 holes in the Australian Open was 'Mr Consistency', Robert Allenby, and at Royal Melbourne in the penultimate event of the year, the Johnnie

(Above) Robert Allenby headed the Order of Merit in 1992; (left) three wins for Craig Parry

when Craig added the Australian PGA Championship to the Australian Masters title he won earlier in the year. Apart from Parry's convincing three stroke victory the major talking point at the PGA in Sydney was an incredible third round 10 under par 61 by Mike Harwood - easily the highlight of what was an otherwise disappointing year for the 6' 4" Sydneyite.

Parry was unable to retain his form the following week in the Heineken Australian

Walker Classic, he swapped 'consistency' for 'brilliance' by destroying a high class international field to win by five strokes with rounds of 66-68-69-72. At one stage in the final round he led the championship by nine strokes. His win proved just how much he had progressed in only his first year as a professional and it is fair to say that the manner of his triumph, and the fact that it enabled him to head the year's Order of Merit, sent shock waves around the golfing world - and they were still reverberating when 'jolly Rodger' earned himself a nice Christmas bonus at Coolum with that dazzling 65 in the year's final event.

THE 1992 HEINEKEN AUSTRALIAN OPEN

everal of the best golfers in the Northern Hemisphere descended on The Lakes Golf Club in Sydney last November to play in the most important championship of the Southern Hemisphere and it was won by a player whose heart is said to belong somewhere in between.

Ever since Steve Elkington was a student golf prodigy in the early 1980s, the 29-year-old Australian has based himself in Houston, Texas. True, there was a brief flirtation with the European Tour in 1986 but he has an American wife and has made a home (and quite a name) for himself in America. Not one to blow his own trumpet, Elkington has been a major force on the US Tour for the past three seasons. In 1990 he won the Greater Greensboro Open, in 1991 the prestigious Players Championship at Sawgrass and early in 1992 the Tournament of Champions which, together with two second place finishes (both play-off defeats) helped him finish 12th on last year's PGA Tour Money List.

Thus it was a rising star, and one blessed, according to the golf coaches, with one of the finest swings in the game, who came to Sydney to play in only his fourth Australian Open Championship. The Lakes is widely regarded as one of the toughest courses in Australia. It has now staged the Australian Open three times, the two previous occasions being in 1964, when Jack Nicklaus won the first of his six titles, and in 1980 when Greg Norman won the first of his three: 'The Bear', 'The Shark' and now 'The Elk' - and how many one wonders will his first victory lead to?

Nicklaus and Norman were prodigiously long hitters when they won their titles (Greg of course still is) and this is another feature of Elkington's game; it is one which certainly contributed to his being able to tame The Lakes, something that many of the big Australian stars fail to do: Rodger Davis, Ian Baker-Finch and Peter Senior all surprisingly

Steve Elkington wins in style at The Lakes

failed to make the half-way cut, as did the pre-championship favourite - following his win the previous week in the Australian PGA - Craig 'four putts' Parry. So who was there to challenge the 'All American' Aussie?

Among the home players there was

Wayne Grady played superbly for two days – then frequented the rough

Wayne Grady, the 1990 US PGA champion and the 21-year-old Rookie sensation Robert Allenby, who would go on to win the Australasian Tour Order of Merit title; then there were the aforementioned stars from the Northern Hemisphere, led by Major winners, Ray Floyd and Mark Calcavecchia from America and Ryder Cup players, Colin Montgomerie and Steven Richardson from Europe. In total 21 overseas players competed in the 1992 Heineken Australian Open: a quality field for a quality championship.

Birdie - birdie - birdie: that is how Wayne Grady began his challenge on the first day, signing eventually for a 67 and a share of the lead, and on the second day he repeated his triple birdie start en route to a marvellous 66 and a four stroke lead after 36 holes. It was a blistering pace for such a demanding course and the only other person able to better 70 on both opening days was Elkington who scored 69-68. The rest of the field were beginning to string out. Leading the chasing pack, however, was 50-year-old Ray Floyd, a great supporter of Australian golf (70-68); Australian Peter McWhinney

(67-72) and Fijian golfer Vijay Singh (70-69). Colin Montgomerie had looked impressive on the first day, scoring a very solid 69, but started to fall away in the second round and the only other player who would feature in the final two days (thanks to a 68 on Saturday) was American Duffy Waldorf - not the most familiar of names perhaps, but a winner of more than half a million dollars on the US Tour in 1992 (no wonder Elkington bases himself there!)

The third round turned out to be the most significant of the championship for it saw a seven stroke swing between Grady and Elkington. Once the most consistent of players, Grady stumbled to a 76 while Elkington returned an almost flawless 69 to take a three stroke advantage into the final round.

It was an advantage he wouldn't squander - ultimately at least - although in strengthening winds, and with the prize of a first Australian Open Championship in sight, he did find it tough going and did well, in the circumstances, to hold his game together. Grady made a final bid on the first nine holes of the last round, reaching the turn in

33 but again collapsed on the back nine, coming home in 41. McWhinney and Waldorf emerged as Elkington's closest pursuers over the closing holes but a par at the last was sufficient for Elkington to score a 74 and win with a couple of shots to spare. It had been a hard-fought but hugely popular victory. And it meant a lot to Elkington, 'I'm tickled pink,' he said, 'And very emotional. It is not often I get home and it really is a great feeling to win in front of the Australian public. I shall leave the trophy with my parents at Woolongong because it belongs in this country.' Well said: scratch a Texan, you see, and there's a true-blue Aussie underneath.

(Above) American Ray Floyd came fifth in an event he regularly supports; (below) a 'tickled' Steve Elkington poses with the famous trophy

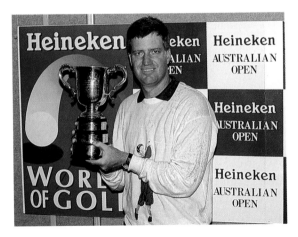

THE 1992 AUSTRALASIAN TOUR

13 - 16 February
AUSTRALIAN MASTERS
HUNTINGDALE, MELBOURNE

C Parry	72	76	67	68	283	Aus$126,581
G Norman	69	70	71	76	286	75,948
J Morse	73	73	69	72	287	47,819
L Stephen	75	68	75	70	288	25,316
G Hjertstedt	70	75	71	72	288	25,316
D Feherty	79	70	67	72	288	25,316
M Colandro	75	69	71	73	288	25,316
B Hughes	75	68	68	77	288	25,316
P Senior	70	75	66	77	288	25,316
P Moloney	74	71	75	69	289	17,229
R Davis	74	72	73	70	289	17,229
R Mackay	69	73	71	76	289	17,229

19 - 22 November
FORD AUSTRALIAN PGA CHAMPIONSHIP
CONCORD, SYDNEY

C Parry	67	67	67	68	269	Aus$ 54,000
P McWhinney	67	67	67	71	272	32,400
B Hughes	70	67	68	68	273	17,400
M Harwood	70	70	61	72	273	17,400
P Fowler	70	68	70	67	275	12,000
I Baker-Finch	67	68	72	69	276	10,350
B Ogle	70	67	69	70	276	10,350
J Morse	66	70	69	72	277	8,850
D Iwasaki-Smith	69	70	66	72	277	8,850

26 - 29 November
HEINEKEN AUSTRALIAN OPEN
THE LAKES, SYDNEY

S Elkington	69	68	69	74	280	Aus$ 144,000
P McWhinney	67	72	70	73	282	70,400
D Waldorf	73	70	68	71	282	70,400
W Grady	67	66	76	74	283	38,400
R Floyd	70	68	73	73	284	32,000

M Allen	72	69	72	72	285	28,800
C Montgomerie	69	72	72	73	286	26,400
F Nobilo	70	72	73	72	287	22,800
J Van de Velde	75	71	69	72	287	22,800
M Ferguson	72	71	73	71	287	22,800
R Allenby	70	73	75	70	288	18,000
T Price	74	73	70	71	288	18,000
V Singh	70	69	78	71	288	18,000

TOURNAMENT · WINNERS

Sanctuary Cove Classic	Rodger Davis
Daikyo Palm Meadows Cup	Ronan Rafferty
The Vines Classic	Ian Baker-Finch
Mercedes Australian Matchplay	Mike Clayton
Pyramid Australian Masters	Craig Parry
AMP New Zealand Open	Grant Waite
CIG New South Wales Open	Craig Parry
Perak Masters	Robert Allenby
Malaysian Masters	Terry Price
Pioneer Singapore PGA	Terry Gale
Air New Zealand/Shell Open	Nick Price
Eagle Blue South Australian Open	Brett Ogle
Ford Australian PGA Championship	Craig Parry
Heineken Australian Open	Steve Elkington
Johnnie Walker Classic	Robert Allenby
Coolum Classic	Rodger Davis

1992 ORDER OF MERIT: TOP 10

1	Robert Allenby	Aus $ 309,063
2	Rodger Davis	276,529
3	Craig Parry	230,839
4	Brad Hughes	196,526
5	Ian Baker-Finch	174,132
6	Brett Ogle	157,113
7	Terry Price	150,378
8	Peter McWhinney	147,981
9	Grant Waite	143,909
10	Peter Senior	133,236

JAPAN

1992 JAPANESE TOUR REVIEW

$\cdots\cdots\cdots\cdots\cdots\cdots\cdots\cdots\cdots\cdots\cdots\cdots\cdots\cdots$

Silly question: what is Japanese for Nick Faldo? Silly answer: Mumbo Jumbo? Uncannily close - although hardly appropriate. Try Masashi Jumbo Ozaki. In 1992 Jumbo dominated golf in Japan in much the way that Faldo dominated in Europe. Both players, physically and metaphorically speaking, towered over their contemporaries; both smashed the previous money records for their respective tours and although neither won before April, each ended the year with six victories.

Jumbo's first success came in the Dunlop International Open where he came from four behind to win a play-off with Canadian Brent Franklin. The following week, four strokes was the margin of his victory as he compiled impressive rounds of 68-69-65-67 to grab the prestigious Crowns title, a tournament won by Seve Ballesteros in 1991 and Greg Norman in 1989.

Ballesteros played in both the Dunlop and Crowns events and Norman, fresh from a spectacular success in the Canadian Open challenged in September's ANA Open, but he also had no answer to Jumbo who (having gained his third victory earlier in the summer) now claimed win number four. The Japan Open Championship, the most coveted prize on the Tour was staged in the same week as the World Matchplay at Wentworth. The respective winners? Ozaki and Faldo, of course, and the word to sum up both victories was 'emphatic'. A superb opening 64 did the trick for Ozaki and his name was being engraved on the trophy long before he holed his final putt.

'But how many of the world's top international players regularly compete on the Japanese circuit?' - that is the jibe frequently directed towards the cream of the PGA Japan Tour; the suggestion being that

(Previous pages) Masashi 'Jumbo' Ozaki; (right) Jumbo's brother, Naomichi 'Joe' Ozaki

week in week out the fields are markedly inferior to those assembled in America and Europe, and hence winning repeatedly isn't quite the feat it appears on paper. (By the end of 1992, 45-year-old Ozaki had won almost 80 times in Japan). The truth is that many leading 'overseas' players - Faldo and Woosnam included - annually, if sporadically, compete in Japan even before the end-of-season International Tour commences. (If only to fulfil contractual obligations to their sponsors!)

The aforementioned International Tour, however, is precisely that - three successive events staged each November just before the curtain closes on the PGA Japan Tour; three events with cosmopolitan fields that collectively wouldn't shame a Major championship. The first of these, the Visa Taiheiyo Club Masters, has been somewhat monopolised in recent years by the Spaniards Ballesteros and Olazabal. The latter was again present in 1992, along with Langer, Watson, Stewart and Mize, and threatened to claim a third title, but in the end the victor, and winner of the scarlet blazer, was you-know-who, Jumbo Ozaki. The Dunlop Phoenix tournament always follows the Taiheiyo Masters. South African David Frost won a play-off last year with Kiyoshi Murota after both finished a stroke ahead of Jumbo's brother, Naomichi 'Joe' Ozaki and the fast-finishing Olazabal, who sank a bunker shot at the 18th for a closing eagle. The final leg of the International Tour, the Casio World Open, saw veteran Isao Aoki gain his second victory of the season and he did it scoring a 66 and a 64 in his middle two rounds.

'Joe' Ozaki was one of a trio of players who won three times on the 1992 Tour, the others being Tommy Nakajima and Massy Kuramoto. Naomichi's most important win of the season came in the lucrative Lark Cup

David Frost wins the Dunlop Phoenix tournament

where he edged out big brother Jumbo by a single stroke. Surprisingly, for the second year in succession, there were no wins for the third member of the Ozaki clan, Tateo 'Jet' Ozaki (a suffering Jet?) and even more surprisingly, four wins for Taiwan's Tze-Ming Cheng. But in Japan at least, 1992 will undoubtedly go down as Jumbo's year. According to the Sony Rankings he's still not among the top dozen golfers in the world. Sony - a Japanese corporation - now that's what I call mumbo jumbo.

JAPAN'S 1992 INTERNATIONAL TOUR

12 - 15 November
VISA TAIHEIYO CLUB MASTERS
TAIHEIYO CLUB, GOTEMBA

M 'Jumbo' Ozaki	74	66	66	70	276	Yen 27,000,000
B Langer	70	70	69	68	277	10,800,000
M Kuramoto	65	68	73	71	277	10,800,000
T Watanabe	73	64	69	71	277	10,800,000
J M Olazabal	70	69	71	68	278	6,000,000
Y Yokoshima	68	75	67	69	279	5,100,000
M Kimura	68	70	69	72	279	5,100,000
K Murota	70	70	69	71	280	4,125,000
T Hamilton	66	74	69	71	280	4,125,000
B Lane	72	72	71	67	282	2,814,000
T Watson	74	70	70	68	282	2,814,000
T C Chen	71	66	73	72	282	2,814,000
R Mackay	75	68	68	71	282	2,814,000
N Yuhara	71	71	71	70	282	2,814,000
J Sluman	74	72	70	67	283	1,980,000
L Mize	74	69	70	70	283	1,980,000
T 'Jet' Ozaki	69	70	69	75	283	1,980,000

Japanese Master 'Jumbo' Ozaki, winner of 1992's Scarlet Jacket at the Taiheiyo Club

M 'Jumbo' Ozaki	68	71	76	69	284	2,640,000
M Kuramoto	71	74	69	70	284	2,640,000
L Mize	69	70	74	71	284	2,640,000
P Senior	72	71	74	68	285	2,016,000
M Brooks	70	73	74	68	285	2,016,000
R Rafferty	71	71	74	69	285	2,016,000
B Franklin	69	71	74	71	285	2,016,000
B Jones	73	68	73	71	285	2,016,000

19 - 22 November
DUNLOP PHOENIX
PHOENIX, MIYAZAKI

D Frost	72	69	69	67	277	Yen 36,000,000
K Murota	68	70	70	69	277	20,000,000
(Frost won playoff at second extra hole)						
N 'Joe' Ozaki	72	70	71	65	278	11,600,000
J M Olazabal	70	72	70	66	278	11,600,000
T Nishikawa	73	71	69	67	280	8,000,000
D Forsman	72	70	72	67	281	6,150,000
F Minoza	72	69	72	68	281	6,150,000
R Gibson	70	72	69	70	281	6,150,000
D Peoples	66	70	72	73	281	6,150,000
D Ishii	74	68	73	67	282	4,300,000
T Watson	72	73	68	69	282	4,300,000
T Lehman	70	70	74	69	283	3,386,000
T Sugihara	73	72	68	70	283	3,386,000
H Meshiai	70	72	69	72	283	3,386,000

26 - 29 November
CASIO WORLD OPEN
IBUSUKI, KAIMONCHO

I Aoki	76	66	64	71	277	Yen 27,000,000
T M Chen	75	71	66	67	279	15,000,000
T Watanabe	74	69	69	68	280	10,200,000
T Lehman	75	72	66	68	281	7,200,000
H Kase	74	69	74	65	282	5,400,000
S Lyle	70	71	72	69	282	5,400,000
K Murota	72	71	69	70	282	5,400,000
P Mickelson	77	69	68	69	283	4,350,000
N Yuhara	76	70	70	68	284	3,120,000
H Meshiai	72	70	72	70	284	3,120,000
T Nakajima	72	67	74	71	284	3,120,000
M Brooks	74	67	70	73	284	3,120,000
Y Mizumaki	70	70	68	76	284	3,120,000

1992 PGA JAPAN TOUR

TOURNAMENT · WINNERS

Daiichi Cup	T. M. Chen
Imperial Open	N. Ozaki
Daido Shizuoka Open	H. Makino
Taylor Made KSB	S. Okuda
Descente Classic	Y. Kaneko
Pocarisweat Open	T. M. Chen
Bridgestone ASO	P. Senior
The Crowns	M. Ozaki
Fuji Sankei Classic	H. Makino
Japan PGA Championship	M. Kuramoto
Pepsi UBE Tournament	T. Nakajima
Mitsubishi Galant	I. Aoki
JCB Sendai Classic	R. Mackay
Sapporo Tokyo Open	N. Yuhara
Yomiuri Sapporo	D. Ishii
Mizuno Open	T. Nakamura
PGA Philanthropy	M. Ozaki
Yonex Hiroshima	N. Yuhara
Nikkei Cup	K. Murota
NST Niigata Open	T. Nakajima
ACOM International	H. Inoue
Maruman Open	T. Hamilton
Daiwa KBC Augusta	T. M. Chen
Japan PGA Matchplay	T. Nakajima
Suntory Open	N. Ozaki
ANA Open	M. Ozaki
Gene Sarazen Jun Classic	T. C. Chen
Tokai Classic	M. O'Meara
Japan Open Championship	M. Ozaki
Asahi Beer Digest	S. Okuda
Bridgestone Open	M. Kuramoto
Lark Cup	N. Ozaki
Visa Taiheiyo Masters	M. Ozaki
Dunlop Phoenix	D. Frost
Casio World Open	I. Aoki
Japan Series of Golf	T. M. Chen
Daikyo Open	M. Kuramoto

LEADING · MONEY · WINNERS

1	Masashi Ozaki	Yen 186,816,466
2	Naomichi Ozaki	130,860,179
3	Tze-Ming Chen	122,317,851
4	Masahiro Kuramoto	116,361,950
5	Tsuneyuki Nakajima	108,674,116
6	Kiyoshi Murota	98,958,726
7	Seiki Okuda	88,944,972
8	Nobumitsu Yuhara	87,420,199
9	Hiroshi Makino	80,972,661
10	Isao Aoki	71,009,733
11	Saburo Fujiki	70,297,628
12	David Ishii	63,273,449
13	Todd Hamilton	62,866,532
14	Tze-Chung Chen	61,678,945
15	Tsukasa Watanabe	59,721,432
16	Toru Nakamura	57,262,408
17	Yoshinori Kaneko	57,230,188
18	Roger Mackay	55,838,229
19	Brent Franklin	53,855,926
20	Tetsu Nishikawa	51,735,257

50 year old Isao Aoki – the Ray Floyd of Japan?
He won twice on the Japanese Tour in 1992

ASIAN & AFRICAN TOURS

1992 ASIAN TOUR

TOURNAMENT · WINNERS

Philippine Open	T-C Wang
Singapore Open	B. Israelson
Hong Kong Open	T. Watson
Malaysian Open	V. Singh
Indian Open	S. Ginn
Thailand Open	B. Ruengkit
Republic of China Open	C-H Lin
Korean Open	T. Hamilton
Dunlop Int. Open	M. Ozaki

ORDER OF MERIT WINNER

Todd Hamilton (USA)

1992 JOHNNIE WALKER ASIAN CLASSIC

Ian Palmer (see European Tour)

1991-2 SAFARI TOUR

TOURNAMENT · WINNERS

Ivory Coast Open	M. Besanceney
Nigerian Open	J. Lebbie
Zimbabwean Open	M. McNulty
Zambian Open	J. Robinson
Kenya Open	A. Bossert

1991 - 1992 SOUTH AFRICA (SUNSHINE) TOUR

TOURNAMENT · WINNERS

Fancourt Hall of Fame	De Wet Basson
Goodyear Classic	J. Hobday
Spoornet Classic	R. Goosen
Protea Ass. South African Open	E. Els
Lexington PGA Championship	E. Els
Bells Cup	D. Feherty
Trustbank Tournament of Champions	B. Lincoln
South African Masters	E. Els
ICL International	K. Johnson
Royal Swazi Classic	E. Els

ORDER OF MERIT

1	Ernie Els	R324,017
2	De Wet Basson	155,425
3	Wayne Westner	147,416
4	Tony Johnstone	109,124
5	Retief Goosen	108,488
6	Derek James	104,318
7	John Bland	91,528
8	Justin Hobday	83,614
9	Bobby Lincoln	82,132

Ernie Els: the new star of Africa

1991-1992 SOUTH AFRICAN TOUR REVIEW

· ·

There is a very strong case for arguing that the most exciting place to be watching golf in 1992 was South Africa. Of course, there were nothing like as many tournaments as were staged in Europe or America, but some of the finishes were quite phenomenal. The reason can be summed up in two words, Ernie Els: a golfing phenomenon. Els was 22 at the start of 1992 and for two years, those 'in the know' had been waiting for him to make his presence felt in the world of professional golf - just as he had done as a brilliant junior and amateur golfer. But surely not even his greatest fans could have predicted he would explode on the scene in such a way.

The Sunshine Tour follows the South African summer, running from December through to early March; the Million Dollar Challenge at Sun City - won in 1992 for the third time in four years by David Frost in controversial circumstances, after Nick Faldo and Nick Price had been disqualified (see chapter one) - doesn't count as an official Tour event (what a short cut that would be to heading the Order of Merit!).

The 1991-1992 season comprised eight tournaments, the first three of which were won by emerging Springbok stars, De Wet Basson (aged 23), Justin Hobday (28) and Retief Goosen (22), who later headed the European Tour qualifying school. The fourth event of the season (and the second of 1992) was the South African Open and it is where Ernie Els decided to come of age. Els won the Tour's biggest event by three strokes and scored a course record 65 in the process. A week later he was also the South African PGA champion; middle rounds of 65-66 having set him up for a handsome victory.

Ireland's David Feherty and South African Bobby Lincoln won the next two events, with Els finishing just two shots behind in the former and missing out on tieing for the latter by just one. The South African Masters followed: the third leg of the South African Open - PGA - Masters treble and Els became only the second player in history, after Gary Player, to win all three in the same season. He did it in great style too, coming from five behind overnight leader Chris Davison with a final round 67.

Els slipped to eighth place in the Sunshine Tour's penultimate event, the ICL International won by Kevin Johnson, but soon rediscovered his winning form to produce an amazing finish to the 1991-1992 South African season. Els had already comfortably won the Order of Merit title when he belatedly entered the Royal Swazi Classic. He opened with a 74, his worst score for many a week, and trailed the aforementioned Davison by nine strokes after the first round. Davison did little wrong for the next three days, scoring 69-66-70, but Els unleashed rounds of 67-64-64 to 'steal' the title from the luckless Davison on the final green. Els, in fact, was four behind with two holes to play but finished eagle - birdie, sinking a 40-foot putt on the last.

When the 1992-1993 season began last December Els picked up where he left off, winning two more South African tournaments before the year-end for a total of six victories in all in 1992. So, the next Gary Player? Not outwardly: he is as tall as Nick Faldo and hits the ball as far as Greg Norman; the rest of the world had just better hope that he doesn't have the 'Man in Black's inner steel.

THE 1992 JOHNNIE WALKER
WORLD CHAMPIONSHIP

● ●

For the second year running the best golfers in the world descended upon the lavish Tryall resort in sunny Jamaica for the final event of the season: an appropriately magical setting in which to see the curtain come down on the golf year. In such surroundings, and at such a time of year, a carnival atmosphere might be excused - if it were not for the fact that 28 players were competing for a pot of $2.7 million with a first prize of $550,000 - never mind the glory of the title, 'World Champion': so, Jamaica, but no 'Dreadlock Holiday'; rather - as things turned out - Jamaica, deadlock final day.

Much time and effort had been expended toughening up the Tryall course in the twelve months since the inaugural Johnnie Walker World Championship in 1991 and it presented a fairly stern challenge in still conditions. For the first three days, however, strong winds made it devilishly difficult and it was by no means the proverbial 'piece of cake' on what turned out to be a sensational Sunday.

Craig Parry was the sole player able to better the par of 70 on the first day, scoring a 68 for a three stroke lead (which he duly surrendered with a 77 in the next round) and only Frost (67), Couples (69) and Kite (69) achieved it on day two. High scores were legion: five of the 28 players failed to break 80 in their opening round and Ballesteros (who eventually finished in last place) scored an 82 in his second. 'Keeping one's head while all about were losing theirs' was the recipe for staying in contention during the first 36 holes. Both Frost and Couples, the defending champion, scored well on the Friday but they had begun on Thursday with rounds of 83 and 77. The three players playing the most consistent golf

'Duelling in Jamaica': Greg Norman watches Nick Faldo drive during the final round

over the first two days were Nick Faldo (71-70); Greg Norman (71-71) and Tom Kite (73-69).

Everything but the weather changed on Saturday as the Open Champion's slender one stroke lead suddenly soared to five after 54 holes. Nick Faldo stormed around the course in 65 strokes, a score that was three better than anyone else could manage that day, and he struck the ball with such authority that it seemed certain that on the final day 27 golfers would be playing for the minor places.... which is exactly what happened, with the one exception of Greg 'he's catchable' Norman. With one round to go Faldo was on 206, Norman on 211 and Kite on 213.

'Blue skies - sixty-five': that is what Norman kept telling himself over and over again when he walked to the first tee for the final round of the 1989 Open at Troon - and then promptly birdied the first six holes in a dazzling 64. And there were blue skies overhead as he walked to the first tee at Tryall. History has a funny knack of repeating itself for now, just as at Troon, Norman started fast, produced a barrage of birdies, was tied after 72 holes but lost out in a play-off. Greg birdied the 1st, 3rd, 4th, 7th, 11th, 13th and 14th at Tryall in the last round, at which point he had actually overtaken his great rival. On the 18th green he was still one ahead of Faldo and his ball was sitting four feet from the flag in two (he had a putt for an incredible 62) while Nick was 16 feet away in the same number. Ever the man for the occasion though, Faldo holed his putt and Norman missed. The rest, as they say, is history. Faldo won the play-off at the first extra hole and the world's number one was duly crowned World Champion - just in time for Christmas.

An Englishman abroad — all except the handkerchief: Nick Faldo with the Johnnie Walker World Championship trophy

17 - 20 December
JOHNNIE WALKER WORLD CHAMPIONSHIP
TRYALL CLUB, JAMAICA

* Nick Faldo (Eng)	71	70	65	68	274	$550,000
Greg Norman (Aus)	71	71	69	63	274	300,000
* Faldo won play-off at 1st extra hole						
Davis Love III (USA)	72	75	70	66	283	165,000
Tom Kite (USA)	73	69	71	70	283	165,000
Ian Woosnam (Wal)	73	71	72	68	284	100,000
Mark Roe (Eng)	71	72	72	70	285	90,000
Fred Couples (USA)	77	69	68	73	287	85,000
David Edwards USA)	73	73	72	70	288	75,000
Raymond Floyd (USA)	73	71	74	70	288	75,000
Tony Johnstone (Zim)	75	73	73	67	288	75,000
Paul Azinger (USA)	75	76	71	67	289	65,000
Colin Montgomerie (Scot)	74	76	71	70	291	64,000
Sandy Lyle (Scot)	76	71	75	70	292	62,500
Craig Parry (Aus)	68	77	73	74	292	62,500
Christy O'Connor Jnr (Ire)	79	72	69	75	295	61,000
Peter O'Malley (Aus)	71	73	75	77	296	58,500
Bernhard Langer (Ger)	77	76	72	71	296	58,500
Robert Allenby (Aus)	80	73	72	71	296	58,500
Steve Elkington (Aus)	80	75	73	68	296	58,500

SENIOR GOLF REVIEW

E asy life, being one of the round bellies (Lee Trevino's pet name for the golfers of the US Senior Tour). Just look at them, being chauffeured around golf courses in state-of-the-art buggies, only needing to exercise their limbs when they climb out of these golfing

'Cheeky Mex' Lee Trevino won six times in 1992

charabancs to hit shots from velvety, carpet-like fairways. It's a wonder they don't play in slippers. And look at the locations in which they are compelled to ply their trade: the various islands of Hawaii; Desert Mountain, Arizona; Palm Beach, Florida; Puerto Rico. Doesn't your heart bleed for them?

Easy life being Lee Trevino. Easy when you're as good at your trade as he is. 'Super Mex' is the uncrowned king of the Round Bellies (not so much Leader of the Rat Pack as Leader of the Fat Pack). During the early part of 1992 in particular Trevino was in such devastating form that every time he teed

up in a Senior's event people were surprised if he didn't go on to win; not that this happened often during the first half of the season as he reeled of six victories, including three in successive weeks. And when he wasn't winning he was invariably coming second. Whatever conveyance he now uses to transport all those hundreds of thousands of dollars to the bank (the wheel barrow he promised to acquire the moment he turned 50 became redundant long ago) must be buckling under the weight.

The two most important titles Trevino claimed in 1992 were The Tradition at Desert Mountain in early April, where he won a titanic head-to-head battle with that most reluctant of seniors, Jack Nicklaus, and two weeks later the USPGA Senior's Championship at the PGA National, Palm Beach. In June Trevino came close to winning the Senior Players Championship - the one senior Major that has so far eluded his grasp - but had to settle for second behind one of the Tour's newest recruits, 1992 US Ryder Cup captain, Dave Stockton.

From about the middle of June until the end of the year, Trevino rarely produced his brilliant early season form but this, it appears was due chiefly to an aggravated thumb injury. The latter part of the 1992 season was dominated by the Crown Princes of the US Seniors Tour, the likes of Mike Hill, George Archer, Jim Colbert and 'Chuckling' Chi Chi Rodriguez, and by the coming of age - literally - of two new bright senior stars, Ray Floyd and Isao Aoki. But before they appeared on the scene there was the not-so-small matter of the US Senior Open in mid-July at Saucon Valley, Pennsylvania.

The US Senior Open was won by Lee Trevino in 1990 and by Jack Nicklaus in 1991; in 1992 it was won by Larry Laoretti: talk about a Major upset! At the start of the season you could have got better odds on Colin Montgomerie winning the US Open. Pre-Saucon Valley, Larry Laoretti was best known for his perpetual cigar smoking; he had spent the best part of the past 30 years as a 'run of the mill' club pro. It was incredible then that he should win by four strokes from Jim Colbert and finish five ahead of such a formidable quartet as Nicklaus, Player, Stockton and Geiberger. The phrase 'as happy as Larry' took on a new dimension after the 13th US Senior Open.

Meanwhile across the water a fledgling European Senior's Tour was beginning to take shape. Ten senior tournaments were held during 1992 in places as far apart as Ireland, Switzerland and Tunisia. The biggest event being the Senior British Open Championship at Royal Lytham in the last week of July. As with its US counterpart a surprise winner emerged, although South African John Fourie could produce a much more impressive curriculum vitae than Larry Laoretti. Fourie won by three shots from former champions Bob Charles and Neil Coles and from a field that included Gary Player and Arnold Palmer. Fourie went on to win the Tour's first Order of Merit title.

Isao Aoki and Ray Floyd respectively turned 50 in August and September of 1992. Earlier in the year both had won an important tour event on their regular home circuits and it came as no surprise when they achieved what Trevino would doubtless describe as the 'round belly - flat belly double'. Floyd was the more successful of the two, winning three of the seven events he entered including the end-of-season Senior Tour Championship in Puerto Rico. In that

same week Trevino pushed his winnings total for the year through the $1million barrier for the second time in three seasons and claimed the leading money winner's title. As Super Mex once said, 'God must be a Mexican.' But does He wear slippers?

(Above) cigar-smoking Larry Laoretti was a surprise winner of the US Senior Open; (left) Ray Floyd, the Senior Tour's latest superstar

THE 1992 SENIOR MAJORS

2 - 5 April
THE TRADITION
DESERT MOUNTAIN, SCOTTSDALE, ARIZONA

L Trevino	67	69	68	70	274	$120,000
J Nicklaus	65	72	69	69	275	69,000
C C Rodriguez	69	66	71	70	276	57,500
T Aaron	68	73	67	70	278	47,500
B Crampton	71	74	67	67	279	32,866
K Zarley	70	71	70	68	279	32,866
D Stockton	67	71	70	71	279	32,866
D Weaver	69	72	71	68	280	21,732
G Brewer	72	70	69	69	280	21,732
M Hill	66	72	72	70	280	21,732
J C Snead	66	71	70	73	280	21,732

16 - 19 April
USPGA SENIORS' CHAMPIONSHIP
PGA NATIONAL, PALM BEACH, FLORIDA

L Trevino	72	64	71	71	278	$100,000
M Hill	73	70	67	69	279	70,000
C C Rodriguez	70	72	68	70	280	50,000
D Stockton	71	71	68	74	284	35,000
G Player	69	71	75	70	285	27,500
H Henning	72	70	70	74	286	22,500
B Charles	77	71	65	74	287	19,000
A Kelley	74	69	70	74	287	19,000
D Dalziel	70	73	72	73	288	16,000
A Geiberger	77	68	73	73	291	14,500
J Nicklaus	73	68	74	76	291	14,500

11 - 14 June
THE SENIOR PLAYERS CHAMPIONSHIP
TPC OF MICHIGAN, DEARBORN, MICHIGAN

D Stockton	71	67	70	69	277	$150,000
L Trevino	70	70	70	68	278	80,000
J C Snead	65	66	72	75	278	80,000
C C Rodriguez	71	70	70	68	279	60,000
S Hobday	75	65	71	69	280	44,000
T Aaron	66	73	70	71	280	44,000
B Charles	67	69	72	73	281	36,000

9 - 12 July
THE US SENIOR OPEN
SAUCON VALLEY, PENNSYLVANIA

L Laoretti	68	72	67	68	276	$130,000
J Colbert	71	66	73	69	279	65,000
J Nicklaus	70	68	75	67	280	27,207
D Stockton	67	66	77	70	280	27,207
G Player	71	68	71	70	280	27,207
A Geiberger	71	66	71	72	280	27,207
C C Rodriguez	73	69	71	68	281	17,269
J Dent	71	70	73	68	282	14,468
S Hobday	69	68	76	69	282	14,468
J Kiefer	67	71	75	69	282	14,468
J P Cain	73	74	68	68	283	11,790
B Crampton	72	71	70	70	283	11,790
G Gilbert	69	67	73	74	283	11,790
C Lohren	74	71	69	70	284	10,369
D Douglass	73	69	71	71	284	10,369
D Rhyan	70	70	75	70	285	9,429
C Coody	70	68	73	74	285	9,429
F Beard	76	70	73	67	286	8,619
L Trevino	73	67	76	70	286	8,619

23 - 26 July
SENIOR BRITISH OPEN CHAMPIONSHIP
ROYAL LYTHAM AND ST ANNES, LANCASHIRE

J Fourie	75	67	71	69	282	£33,330
B Charles	71	69	72	73	285	17,360
N Coles	69	71	72	73	285	17,360
P Butler	70	71	72	73	286	10,000
T Horton	74	70	69	75	288	7,650
A Toyoda	75	71	70	72	288	7,650
G Player	73	76	69	71	289	5,500
S Hobday	72	72	74	71	289	5,500
A Proctor	72	74	70	74	290	4,250
A Palmer	70	72	72	76	290	4,250
D Douglass	78	70	73	71	292	3,390
J Garaialde	75	74	68	75	292	3,390
J Ferree	76	75	72	70	293	3,180
B Zimmerman	73	73	75	72	293	3,180
C O'Connor	72	72	74	75	293	3,180
J Hirsch	71	72	70	80	293	Am

AMATEUR GOLF REVIEW

· ·

There was a time when one followed amateur golf simply for the sake (and pleasure) of following amateur golf; nowadays it is done as much for the purpose of gazing into the crystal golf ball, to discover clues as to who is likely to achieve a victory on the PGA Tour (as he had done the previous year while still an amateur) but did manage a second place finish in the New England Classic in July.

Almost as big things are being predicted for David Duval, a 1991 Walker Cup team

(Left) Eldrick 'Tiger' Woods, the 16 year old US junior sensation; (right) Vicki Goetze, US Women's champion

star in the world of professional golf in the immediate years to come. It has been so since 'the Coming of the Bear' - Jack Nicklaus - who burst on the scene as an amateur prodigy, twice winning the US Amateur Championship, before turning professional and defeating the world's number one, Arnold Palmer, to win the 1962 US Open, his first professional victory.

In 1992, 21-year-old left-hander Phil Mickelson, the uncrowned 'King of the Amateurs' since the beginning of the decade, turned professional on the eve of the US Open and in his first round as a professional scored a 68 at Pebble Beach. He didn't go on

mate of Phil Mickelson, who led a 1992 Tour event for three days before collapsing in the final round, and for the 1992 US Amateur Champion Justin Leonard, who won his title so convincingly at Muirfield Village (not a bad omen for a start) and dominated the American amateur scene last year. And then what about 16-year-old schoolboy, Eldrick 'Tiger' Woods, son of a black father and Thai mother who competed in the Los Angeles Open? As for future LPGA stars it seems one needn't hunt further than Vicki Goetze who captured her second US Women's Amateur Championship in 1992. Vicki was all of 19 years of age.

Spinning our crystal golf ball, just as every precocious American golfer is labelled (or lumbered) with the billing of 'the next Nicklaus' so every Australian prodigy is now heralded as the next Greg Norman; every South African as the next Gary Player and every New Zealander as the next Bob Charles. Nineteen ninety-two may well have seen the emergence of genuine successors to Norman and Player in the form of Ernie Els and Robert Allenby, while the remarkable victory of New Zealand in the World Amateur Team Championship in Vancouver would suggest that New Zealand is producing some exceptional young talent. The rising Kiwi stars to look out for are Phil Tataurangi and Mike Campbell, both are of Maori descent.

In Europe an 18-year-old Scotsman (Stephen Dundas) defeated a 19-year-old Welshman (Bradley Dredge) to win the 1992 Amateur Championship at Carnoustie, while Denmark's Pernille Pedersen narrowly triumphed over England's Joanne Morley at Saunton in the Women's Amateur.

Arguably the brightest future talent in Europe, however, is to be found in Sweden and Spain. In 1991 a Spaniard, Francisco Valera, won the British Boys Championship (following in the footsteps of José-Maria Olazabal) and last year the final was contested by two Swedes, Leif Westerberg and Frederick Jacobson: Westerberg won the 1992 title but Jacobson went on to win the European and World Boy's Championships. Probably the most resounding win in European amateur golf in 1992 was Ignacio Garrido's nine-shot victory in the Brabazon Trophy at Hollinwell and the most surprising being the success of the Spanish team in the women's World Amateur Team Championship in Canada. The leading women's amateur player in Europe in 1992 was Sweden's Annika Sorenstam, who won the individual title in the above-mentioned World Amateur Team Championship and who was beaten by Vicki Goetze in the final of the US Women's Amateur at Kemper Lakes. Not everything went right for Goetze in 1992 though; she was a member of the American Curtis Cup team who surrendered the Cup to Great Britain and Ireland at Hoylake last summer.

So the Curtis Cup is back in the Old World. Will the Walker Cup in 1993 produce a similar result? Alas our crystal ball is beginning to flicker and fade....

Claire Hourihane of Great Britain & Ireland in action during the Curtis Cup at Hoylake

27TH CURTIS CUP

· ·

Royal Liverpool, Hoylake, Cheshire, England

DAY ONE

FOURSOMES (GB&I first):
J Hall & C Hall halved with A Fruhwirth & V Goetze;
V Thomas & C Lambert bt
    L Shannon & S Le Brun Ingram 2&1;
J Morley & C Hourihane bt T Hanson
    & C Semple Thompson 2&1

SINGLES:
Morley halved with Fruhwirth;
J Hall lost to Goetze 3&2;
E Farquharson bt R Weiss 2&1;
N Buxton lost to M Lang 2 down;
Lambert bt Semple Thompson 3&2;
C Hall bt Shannon 6&5

DAY TWO

FOURSOMES:
J Hall & C Hall halved with Fruhwirth & Goetze;
Hourihane & Morley halved with Lang & Weiss;
Lambert & Thomas lost to Hanson & Semple Thompson 3&2

SINGLES:
Morley bt Fruhwirth 2&1;
Lambert bt Hanson 6&5;
Farquharson lost to Le Brun Ingram 2&1;
Thomas lost to Shannon 2&1;
Hourihane lost to Lang 2&1;
C Hall bt Goetze 1 up

MATCH RESULT: GB&I 10, USA 8

Prince Andrew presents the Curtis Cup to the victorious Great Britain & Ireland team

THE AMATEUR & US AMATEUR CHAMPIONSHIPS

August 31 - September 5
1992 AMATEUR CHAMPIONSHIP
CARNOUSTIE, ANGUS, SCOTLAND

QUARTER-FINALS:
S Dundas beat M Meehan (USA) 3 and 1
S Gallacher beat H McKibbin 2 holes
M Stanford by 1 Garbutt 3 and 2
B Dredge beat L Westwood 1 hole
SEMI-FINALS:
S Dundas beat S. Gallacher 4 and 3
B Dredge beat M Stanford 4 and 3
FINAL (36-holes):
S DUNDAS beat B DREDGE 7 and 6

August 25 - 31
92ND US AMATEUR
MUIRFIELD VILLAGE, OHIO

QUARTER-FINALS:
J Leonard beat D White 2 and 1
A Doyle beat G Zahringer 1 up
K Mitchum beat M Stone at 19th
T Scherrer beat J Harris 4 and 3
SEMI-FINALS:
J Leonard beat A Doyle 2 and 1
T Scherrer beat K Mitchum 3 and 2
FINAL (36 holes):
J LEONARD beat T SCHERRER 8 and 7

Amateur champion Steve Dundas plays a deft bunker shot at Carnoustie

June 10 - 14
1992 WOMEN'S AMATEUR CHAMPIONSHIP
SAUNTON, DEVON

QUARTER-FINALS:
P Pedersen (Denmark) beat L Walton 4 and 3
C Lambert beat K D'Algue (France) 4 and 3
T Eakin beat T Samuel (Canada) at 19th
J Morley beat C Semple Thompson (US) 1 hole
SEMI-FINALS:
P Pedersen beat C Lambert 1 hole
J.Morley beat T Eakin 3 and 2
FINAL
P PEDERSEN beat J MORLEY 1 hole

August 10 - 15
92ND US WOMEN'S AMATEUR CHAMPIONSHIP
KEMPER LAKES, ILLINOIS

QUARTER-FINALS:
V Goetze beat T Hanson 4 and 3
A Sorenstam (Sweden) beat M A Pearson 7 and 5
C Semple Thompson beat A Fruhwirth 1 hole
P Cornett-Iker beat E Port 2 holes
SEMI-FINALS:
A Sorenstam beat P Cornett-Iker 7 and 6
V Goetze beat C Semple Thompson 5 and 4
FINAL
V GOETZE beat A SORENSTAM 1 hole

1993
A YEAR TO SAVOUR

....

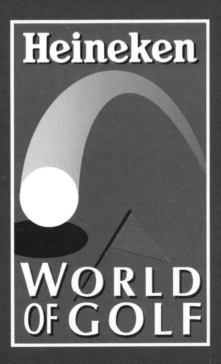

JANUARY

Glaringly obvious: the unmistakable silhouette of
Payne Stewart hits into the sun against the unmistakable
back-drop of Pebble Beach.

California, Hawaii and Arizona is where the US PGA Tour begins its 1993 schedule and it is quite possible that a
player will have won in excess of half a million dollars before the month is out: in the mid-1970s Johnny Miller
once began a season with three straight wins. The PGA European Tour also commences in January with
the first ever Madeira Island Open then after a gap of a few weeks comes the Dubai Desert Classic.
Elsewhere in the world there is the South African PGA, and in Australia, the Heineken Classic
at The Vines Resort near Perth.

FEBRUARY

· ·

Well at least he missed all the bunkers!
Sand and people encircle the third green at Huntingdale,
home of the Australian Masters.

Coming relatively soon after his magnificent 63 in Jamaica, the likely favourite at Huntingdale in February
will be Greg Norman. The Great White Shark has won the Australian Masters no fewer than six times, most
recently in 1990 when he got the better of Nick Faldo in an exciting final day's play. February is also the
month of the New Zealand Open at Paraparaumu Beach, near Wellington and the Hong Kong Open at Royal
Hong Kong. The US Tour spends the entire month in California while the European Tour visits the essentially
non-European outposts of Singapore and Morocco before anchoring in Tenerife.

MARCH

· ·

Six gentlemen of Gerona: golfers and caddies make
their way through the early morning dew following an early start
in the 1992 Catalan Open.

In 1993 the Catalan Open (now the Heineken Open Catalonia) moves to April and the biggest event of the
month on the European Tour is the Mediterranean Open at El Saler, scene of Bernhard Langer's incredible 62
in the 1984 Spanish Open. On the other side of the Atlantic, Florida is where most of the action is to be found
and America's newest superstar, Davis Love will be looking to repeat his 1992 win in the
Players Championship at the TPC at Sawgrass.

APRIL

If there is one golf course in the world
that is prettier than the US Masters course at Augusta
it is surely the par three course at Augusta.

Between 8 - 11 April (Easter weekend) the eyes of the golfing world are sure to be dazzled - and not just by
the kaleidoscope of colours - as the 57th Masters tournament unfolds. Fred Couples ended the great run of
European victories last year; perhaps 1993 will be Australia's year? There are two 'Senior Majors' in April
and as for golf in Europe, the Volvo Tour rarely journeys far from the Mediterranean and ends the month
in Barcelona with the Heineken Open Catalonia at El Montanya.

MAY

· ·

The superb par three 11th on the Jack Nicklaus Course at St Mellion
in Cornwall; the construction team had to move 'heaven and earth'
to create this hole: note the strategic positioning of the church.

St Mellion hosts the twenty third Benson & Hedges International
tournament at the beginning of May, the year's first European
Tour event to be staged on English soil; later in the same month
comes the Volvo PGA Championship at Wentworth. In Japan there
are two important events, the Crowns Tournament and the
Japanese PGA Championship, while the biggest event on the US
Tour is the Byron Nelson Classic in Texas.

JUNE

·······································

A vision in blue and green: the par three 12th
at Muirfield Village, Ohio is one of the most famous short holes
in the world of golf.

Muirfield Village, like St Mellion opposite, was designed by
Nicklaus, and it too stages an important tour event, namely the
Memorial. In June this year Arnold Palmer is to be honoured at
the event. Two weeks later the US Open (17-20) returns to
Baltusrol for the first time since 1980 (when Nicklaus won) and
to keep the Golden Bear theme running, also in June, Mt. Juliet,
Jack's first Irish design, hosts the Carrolls Irish Open.

CHAPTER · FIVE

JULY

· ·

Not so much a damsel, as a maiden in distress.
A violent storm hit Sandwich during the 1985 Open. This view is
from behind the 6th, the famous 'Maiden'

Traditional links golf dominates during July with the Open Championship at Royal St Georges, Sandwich (15-18)
being followed immediately by the Heineken Dutch Open at Noordwijkse: Nick Faldo will be defending the
former, Bernhard Langer, the latter. The European Tour does especially well for venues in July for there is also
the Scottish Open at Gleneagles. In America the prestigious Western Open takes place in July, as do both the
US Women's Open and the US Senior Open.

AUGUST

·······························

**America's Bob Tway has just holed a bunker shot
and broken the heart of Australian Greg Norman in the 1986 USPGA
Championship at Inverness.**

The US PGA Championship returns to Inverness (12-15) but Bob Tway is unlikely to be one of the favourites; Greg Norman probably will be, however, as will the two 'overseas Nicks', Price, the defending champion and Faldo, the World Champion. Also in America there is the Walker Cup at Interlachen and in Europe the Women's British Open at Woburn.

SEPTEMBER

· ·

'Now for that big American breakfast!'
Spanish Masters, Seve Ballesteros and José-Maria Olazabal
traditionally save their best form for the Ryder Cup

No event is more eagerly awaited than the Ryder Cup (24-26) and, if the last five encounters are anything
to go by, no event is likely to be more evenly and keenly contested! Both Ballesteros and Olazabal had
disappointing seasons in 1992 but the prospect of taking on the Americans is likely to inspire them long before
September comes. Two important European Tour events also occur in September: the European Masters amid
the Swiss mountains at Crans and the European Open at the superb new East Sussex National.

OCTOBER

·····································

**'Jumbo' Ozaki is the Arnold Palmer of Japanese golf:
he has his own army of hero-worshipping fans, attacks courses and
wins tournaments like they were going out of fashion**

Jumbo Ozaki, will very probably start as favourite for the 1993 Japan Open in October, it being one of six events he won in 1992. Another likely favourite and defending champion will be Nick Faldo at Wentworth in the World Matchplay Championship. St Andrews hosts the Alfred Dunhill Cup in October; Paul Azinger will be hoping for a repeat win in America's Tour Championship and on the other side of the world the Australasian Tour recommences in South East Asia.

NOVEMBER

· ·

'Golf takes us to such beautiful places,'
said Henry Longhurst: Lake Nona in Florida enjoys an
idyllic (Wish You Were Here) setting

In the second week of November Lake Nona stages the 1993 World Cup Golf by Heineken. It is the event's 40th anniversary year and America will be looking to retain a trophy they won in dramatic circumstances at La Moraleja, Spain. One week earlier, in Europe, the Volvo Tour reaches its climax with the Volvo Masters at Valderrama; and towards the end of the month a strong international field will assemble for the Heineken Australian Open Championship at the Metropolitan Golf Club in Melbourne.

DECEMBER

· ·

In golf everything is possible: despite the
green carpet-like fairways the famous PGA West Course in California
was carved out of near-desert terrain

Australia, Japan and South Africa provide the main focus for tournament golf in December, although the
US Senior Tour now intrudes well into December. Skins Games, Shoot Outs and million dollar challenges
prevent the stars of the European and American Tours from becoming too idle or rusty and only a few days
before Christmas comes the Johnnie Walker World Championship in Jamaica, or as it became in 1992,
the Nick Faldo - Greg Norman show.

1993 MAJORS

A preview by Richard Dyson

If the quality of the courses on which they are to be played is anything to go by, then the 1993 Major championship season should be a vintage one indeed. There can be no complaints this time of any of the four venues having dubious credentials for staging the game's most prestigious events, as occasionally there have been in recent years.

Augusta National, Baltusrol, Royal St Georges and Inverness are all long established and regular Major sites that truly measure up to the honour bestowed upon them. The calibre of the champions these classic tests of the game have previously produced bears witness to their suitability to the task, while their historical traditions are the very essence of what the Majors are all about.

So the season will have a familiar feel but will surely be no less exciting for that. As always it all begins in early April when Augusta National will stage its 57th Masters Tournament.

Last year Britain's remarkable run of four consecutive wins ended when laid-back Fred Couples, justifying his 'World Champion' billing, became the first home winner of the green jacket since Larry Mize's dramatic

Augusta in all its glory: Bernhard Langer and Greg Norman try to read between the lines

Nick Faldo will be going for a third Masters title in April; let's hope he finds time to smell the flowers along the way

triumph in 1987. It was a win greeted with relief as much as anything by the increasingly patriotic American galleries who had endured more than enough European success of late.

Couples and his fellow countrymen will be anxious to make sure his victory was not just a one-off interruption of European dominance; the Europeans, for their part, will be equally keen to make sure it was exactly just that. With the players from the rest of the world to consider as well (led by a highly talented group of Australians desperate for a first Masters success) it is clear that everyone will have something to prove when the action opens at Augusta this year. Whoever triumphs though, the idyllic setting of Bobby Jones' dream course is always the real winner at The Masters.

A touch of irony at this year's Masters will be provided by the arrival of a certain Thomas O. Kite Jnr. Despite an enviable record of consistency over the years at Augusta, Kite was not afforded an invite to last year's event, much to his own disappointment and to general amazement. This year as he drives down Magnolia Lane as reigning US Open Champion he could be forgiven for wearing a rather smug look, but that, of course, wouldn't be in the nature of the man.

Now Tom has experienced Major glory he is keen for more and he would be more than happy to emulate Curtis Strange's feat in 1989 (aided by his own infamous final day collapse at Oak Hill) of retaining the US Open. His chance will come this June in Springfield, New Jersey when Baltusrol stages its record seventh National Championship (one more than Oakmont).

The 93rd US Open will be played over the Lower Course, an A. W. Tillinghast design (along with the Upper Course) of over 70 years ago, though bearing modifications made by Robert Trent Jones for the first of its three US Opens in 1954. It boasts one of the longest and most demanding finishes in the game. The par five 17th, at 630 yards the longest hole in the history of the US Open and featuring the notorious 'Sahara Desert' cross bunkers, is followed by the par five 18th, a 542-yard, stream-lined, dog-leg left to a tightly guarded green.

The most famous hole on the course, however, is the short 4th. It isn't especially long at just under 200 yards but involves a carry over water all the way to a shallow green backed by bunkers and banked at its front with a stone wall.

When Trent Jones was challenged that he'd made this hole too difficult for the 1954 US Open field he promptly went out to try it himself and holed in one! (a feat emulated by Tom Watson in the first round of Baltusrol's last US Open thirteen years ago).

What a championship that 1980 US Open proved to be. Who will ever forget how Jack Nicklaus edged out the plucky Japanese golfer Isao Aoki to join Willie Anderson, Bobby Jones and Ben Hogan as a record four-time winner of the event. It was a week in which records galore were set, the most notable being first round 63s by Nicklaus and Tom Weiskopf (still the lowest rounds ever in the US Open, equalling Johnny Miller's score at Oakmont seven years earlier) and a record low winning score of 272 by Nicklaus.

It was not the first time the Golden Bear had won a US Open at Baltusrol, nor, indeed, set a record low aggregate there, having previously achieved these deeds in 1967 - so what price a third consecutive US Open victory over the Lower Course for Jack this year? If that may be stretching the imagination somewhat, the odds on a European success will be considerably shorter, for in rapidly changing times the US Open has remained, for over a decade, the last bastion of American Major dominance. The last overseas winner was Australia's David Graham at Merion in 1981 while for Europe's last victory one has to go back all of 23 years to Tony Jacklin's success at Hazeltine.

Jack Nicklaus with the US Open trophy at Baltusrol in 1980: it was the Golden Bear's record equalling fourth (and final?) win in the event

Colin Montgomerie raised European hopes last year with a gallant third place finish but this time perhaps no one will be more determined than Seve Ballesteros, for the Spaniard has a big score to settle. After winning his first Masters title in 1980 he came to Baltusrol harbouring Grand Slam aspirations but ended up being ignominiously disqualified for arriving late for a second round tee off time.

Come July, when the Open Championship returns to Royal St. Georges after a gap of eight years, it will be most unlikely that anyone is still in with a chance of that elusive Grand Slam, for only Palmer and Nicklaus have previously arrived in Britain with their hopes still intact. Yet for most, winning the 122nd Open itself will be the ultimate dream.

It will be the twelfth time the Open has been played over this famous Kent links, the first being 99 years ago when J. H. Taylor became the first English professional to win

Sandy Lyle holes a crucial putt at the 15th on his way to winning the Open at Royal St Georges in 1985

the title. Since then such illustrious names as Vardon and Hagen (both twice), Cotton and Locke have triumphed here.

For Sandy Lyle this year's Open will bring back many happy memories of his first Major victory. The 1985 Open was not a classic but will always be memorable for British golf as the popular Scot became the first home winner for 16 years.

After dropping a shot on the final hole, when his attempted chip from Duncan's Hollow rolled agonisingly back to his feet, Sandy had to endure an uncomfortable wait

before being confirmed as champion. It was his consecutive final round birdies on two of the most difficult holes, the notorious par five 14th (Suez Canal) and the long par four 15th, that proved decisive.

Though the course isn't exactly everyone's cup of tea and Jack Nicklaus has described it as his least favourite Open venue, such criticism is somewhat undeserved, for it is undoubtedly a layout that will fully test the world's best players.

With only Mark Calcavecchia's win at Royal Troon in 1989 in the last nine years, the Americans will be keen to improve on their recent Open record. Payne Stewart, a redoubtable Open performer and runner-up at Royal St. Georges last time, will be perhaps their leading hope.

However, a European victory is more likely to be on the cards. Seve Ballesteros goes for his fourth Open on the course where he won the 1983 Sun Alliance PGA while Bernhard Langer has top three finishes to his credit in the last two Opens at Sandwich.

British hopes will be especially high with Sandy Lyle, the defending champion over the course, and Nick Faldo defending his title, won in such heart-stopping fashion at Muirfield last year.

With three wins in the last six years, Faldo is assembling an Open record to match Tom Watson, whose five wins came in just nine years. Also like Watson, Faldo is finding success north of the border easier to come by, but a first victory on home soil could be a strong possibility over the links where, in 1980, he won his third PGA title.

So to the final Major of the year, the 75th US PGA Championship, which is to be staged in August at the Inverness club at Toledo, Ohio. Not that the PGA of America originally scheduled it this way.

All calm at Inverness - historic venue for the 1993 USPGA Championship.

Aronimink in Pennsylvania, where 31 years ago Gary Player won his first USPGA title, was to have staged the event. However, the suburban Philadelphia course was replaced when it refused to change its membership policies.

So Inverness it is and that means an early return to the venue which saw such a dramatic conclusion to the 1986 USPGA, when Bob Tway holed his famous bunker shot at the last hole to deny the unfortunate Greg Norman.

The last twenty years have seen only three overseas wins but two of these (Wayne Grady in 1990 and a deserved first Major victory for Nick Price at Bellerive last year) have come in the last three years, so America's hold on the splendid Wanamaker Trophy is definitely slipping.

No European has ever won the PGA title but the omens, particularly for a British success, are good. After all, the club bears a Scottish name, Scots architect Donald Ross played an important role in the early design of the course and the first Major winner at Inverness was pipe-smoking, big-hitting Ted Ray who won the 1920 US Open when fellow Channel Islander Harry Vardon

suffered a dramatic late collapse in the face of a gale.

Inverness' three subsequent US Open winners, Billy Burke in 1931, Dick Mayer in 1957 and Hale Irwin in 1979, were all able to meet the course's demands for great accuracy, both from the tee and to its small greens. Nick Faldo's game certainly suits such requirements and he will be keen to go one better than his joint runner-up spot last year.

Indeed Faldo is perhaps the only name one could venture forward as a probability, as opposed to a possibility, for Major success in 1993. There are many possibilities of course, but in view of the fact that the last two years have each produced three first-time winners, it is perhaps to those players still hungry for a Major breakthrough that one should look for success this year.

That means the likes of Love, Cook, Azinger, Elkington, Frost, Montgomerie, McNulty and Parry but principally José-Maria Olazabal. The young Spaniard is now under even greater pressure as Tom Kite's successor to the unwanted tag of best player never to have won a Major, but if he adds more patience to his exceptional skills then 1993 could be his year at last.

1993 could be
José-Maria
Olazabal's year

1993 HEINEKEN WORLD OF GOLF

· ·

A Preview by David MacLaren

It goes almost without saying that the most coveted quartet of tournaments in professional golf is the Grand Slam. Together, the Open Championship, the Masters, US Open and USPGA Championship remain the pinnacle of every professional golfer's aspirations, as well as providing the focus to the golfing year for armchair enthusiasts. However, whilst the Grand Slam remains outside the domain of commercial sponsorship, there is another group of top-rank tournaments which, through being brought together under the Heineken umbrella, seem destined to obtain the kind of stature reserved only for championships of the very highest calibre.

Heineken's worldwide involvement in professional golf in 1993 includes the sponsorship of five principal tournaments: the Heineken Australian Open, the Heineken Classic (formerly The Vines Classic), the Heineken Dutch Open, the Heineken Open Catalonia and the World Cup Golf by Heineken - five events that span the spectrum of international tournament play, with different types of course, different fields and different demands.

When it was announced during the 1992 World Cup at La Moraleja that Heineken was to take over main sponsorship of the tournament from American multi-national Philip Morris, it marked a new and exciting

In its 40th Anniversary year, The World Cup Golf by Heineken will be staged in November at Lake Nona in Florida

chapter for golf's most enduring and prestigious team competition. The previous sponsor had supported the event since 1988 and had worked hard to ensure that the World Cup regained its rightful place at the summit of team competition. Now, with the aid of Heineken's resources, world-wide recognition and five-year commitment, the World Cup can look forward to a secure and challenging future.

deprived of a memorable double triumph by the formidable Australian duo of Peter Thomson and Kel Nagle, who were themselves beaten into second place in 1955 by the first of the succession of American victories.

Then, as now, the World Cup was as important in golfing circles as the football version is to soccer fans, and the world's best players were invariably lured by the

The 3rd green (with the short 4th hole in the background) at Lake Nona, Florida

Inaugurated in 1953, the Canada Cup, as it was called until 1966, was unsurprisingly first played in Montreal. Hopes of a home victory by the Canadian pairing of Leonard and Kerr were only thwarted by the Argentinean team led by the incomparable Roberto De Vicenzo, who triumphed with a two round aggregate of 287. The tournament was extended to four rounds for each player the following year and Argentina were only

opportunity to represent their countries in a truly global tournament. For sheer star quality, one need look no further than the 1956 tournament, played at Wentworth, which saw the American team of Ben Hogan and Sam Snead triumph over the South African duo of Bobby Locke and Gary Player.

Founded with the laudable intention of spreading international goodwill, the impartial spectator could be forgiven for

(Right) Steve Elkington will defend his Heineken Australian Open title at Metropolitan in November; (below) Australia's new star, Robert Allenby

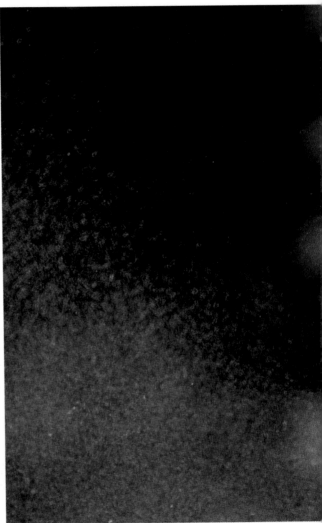

thinking that this message has been ignored in the United States, with the Americans clocking up a staggering 18 victories in the tournament, culminating in the 1992 double birdie finish by the new US dream team of Fred Couples and Davis Love III.

It would be wrong to think of the World Cup solely in competitive terms, and the continuing success of the tournament is due as much to the opportunity it affords to golfers from developing golfing nations to pit their skills against the world's best as to the departure from the usual grind of 72-hole

The elegant swing of Ian Baker-Finch who won The Vines (now Heineken) Classic in 1992

individual strokeplay events. As in every major sport, politics has periodically cast its unwanted shadow over the game of golf, as for instance when the South African team was forced to withdraw on the eve of the 1976 World Cup due to anti-apartheid sanctions imposed by the United Nations. By and large, however, the World Cup has succeeded in regaining the prestige of its early years, and the combination of Heineken's involvement and the the majestic Tom Fazio-designed Lake Nona in Florida should ensure that the 1993 event builds on the success of previous years.

If the World Cup Golf by Heineken deserves its place among the elite events of team golf, the Heineken Australian Open has few peers as an individual championship coveted by the world's top professionals. One need look no further for proof of the tournament's credibility than the mid 1970s when Jack Nicklaus won the title three times in four years. Other American superstars such as Arnold Palmer, Ray Floyd, Tom Watson and Mark Calcavecchia have also left their indelible mark on the championship, with the home flag being flown by, among others, David Graham, Peter Senior, three-time winner Greg Norman and most recently Steve Elkington.

In 1993 the Heineken Australian Open returns to Melbourne; more particularly to one of that city's revered sand-belt courses, namely The Metropolitan Golf Club. The championship was last staged at Metropolitan in 1979 when Jack Newton held off the spirited challenge of a young Greg Norman. Like its famous neighbours, which include Royal Melbourne and Kingston Heath, Metropolitan has a feel reminiscent of the best inland courses in England, such as Sunningdale and Woodhall Spa. Peter Thomson (another Australian Open winner at Metropolitan) once said of the layout: 'It is no exaggeration to say that this course is comparable with anything in the world.' Rich praise indeed.

The Heineken Classic (formerly The Vines Classic) will be contested in January at the magnificent Vines Resort near Perth. Nineteen ninety-three marks the first year of Heineken's involvement, and it is to be hoped that the tournament produces a final day to rival that of 1992, when the elegant Ian Baker-Finch eventually staggered over the victory tape. The then reigning Open Champion held a two shot lead going into the 16th of the final round, but unsound club selection at the par three resulted in a watery grave and a seemingly fatal double-bogey. The penultimate hole also threatened disaster, until the wilting Australian managed to salvage a par, before courageously sinking a perilous eight-foot birdie putt on the last to see off American Jeff Maggert and New Zealander Frank Nobilo by a single shot.

Baker-Finch and the rest of the assembled field were full of praise for the spectacular course. The 27-hole complex lies in the heart of the Swan Valley wine growing area and is less than an hour's drive from Perth. The development comprises houses, apartments and a magnificent country club where tennis, croquet, squash, swimming and other activities vie for the golfer's attention.

One major difference between this and many other sumptuous new golf-related developments is that at The Vines, no effort has been spared to retain as much of the natural bushland setting as possible. The result is a harmonious and attractive resort whose centrepiece is a 27-hole layout with the ability to enthral professional and novice alike. Each nine holes is named after a feature in its layout: Ellen Brook (1-9); the Lakes (10-18) and Wild Flower (19-27). Not surprisingly (although perhaps a little sadistically!) the Lakes is used as the inward half for championships.

The Australian circuit is a popular off-season stop-over for European and American players seeking some winter sunshine after the rigours of their own tours. Golf is very much a global game these days, as exemplified by Heineken's worldwide sponsorship programme, and nowhere is this better demonstrated than with the Heineken Dutch Open, staged at Noordwijkse in Leiden. The last 11 years of an increasingly popular tournament have revealed an international array of champions: two German victories (Bernhard Langer will be the defending champion in 1993), one English, three Scottish, one Australian, two Spanish, one Welsh and one American.

A long, and often unforgiving links course, Noordwijkse has staged six Dutch Opens - eloquent testimony to its ability to stage important championships and to offer a stern test to some of the world's best players. Part of the charm of Noordwijkse is the combination of tall sand dunes with some attractive pine forest. The latter feature first comes into play at the 5th, a dog-leg to the right where the optimum line for the tee shot is to the left, allowing an unimpaired view of the green and reducing the danger caused by a bunker that guards the right side of the green.

The worthy victor of the 1993 Heineken Dutch Open will no doubt be among the most proficient in overcoming the challenge

Pyrenees. As one might imagine, the mountain views are spectacular, especially perhaps those from the beautifully refurbished, traditional Catalan-style clubhouse and the adjacent hotel.

Heineken has been fortunate in associating itself with tournaments that possess both a high profile and which succeed in attracting many of the world's foremost players. Part of the secret clearly lies in the quality of the

The 18th hole at Noordwijkse: a fine finish to a classic test of traditional links golf. Noordwijkse will once again host the Heineken Dutch Open in 1993

posed by this, and other crucial holes, such as the 8th and the notorious 14th which combines a steeply sloping fairway with an encroaching out-of-bounds.

The most recent extension to Heineken's burgeoning presence on the European Tour concerns the former Catalan Open, now the Heineken Open Catalonia, won in 1991 by José-Maria Olazabal and in 1992 by Jose Rivero. In 1993 the tournament is to be played over the striking new El Montanya course which is situated 35 minutes drive north of Barcelona amid the foothills of the

respective venues, and it can be predicted with some certainty that Lake Nona, Metropolitan, The Vines Resort, El Montanya and Noordwijkse will in 1993 produce winners of a sufficient calibre to gladden sponsors, organisers and spectators alike.

HEINEKEN WORLD OF GOLF SCHEDULE
Jan 28-31:   Heineken Classic
April 22-25: Heineken Open Catalonia
July 22-25: Heineken Dutch Open
Nov 11-14:   World Cup Golf by Heineken
Nov 25-28:   Heineken Australian Open

1993 RYDER CUP

· ·

A Preview by Malcolm Hamer

t is difficult to imagine that the drama and the excitement of the Ryder Cup encountered at Kiawah Island in 1991 could ever be repeated. Millions of American and European golf fans, fraught with tension, could hardly bear to watch as Bernhard Langer addressed the final and fateful putt.

But history as usual was repeating itself since there had been two other occasions on which the result depended on the success or failure of the last stroke played in the last match. In 1933, at Southport and Ainsdale, Syd Easterbrook, an Englishman who was never to win a tournament of any note, reached the final green all square with Densmore Shute. The teams were level with five and a half points each. While Shute

putted too strongly and missed the return, Easterbrook was a little short with his approach and was left with a teasing putt of just over a yard with a left to right borrow. He holed out manfully to give Britain the closest of victories. A couple of weeks later Denny Shute gained a sweet revenge by winning the Open Championship at St Andrews after a play-off with his compatriot Craig Wood; Syd Easterbrook finished equal third.

In 1969 the ebb and flow of a remarkable Ryder Cup contest left the two pre-eminent golfers from each side level on the final tee at Royal Birkdale; the two teams were level too, with fifteen and a half points each. Tony Jacklin, sparky and self-confident, the Open Champion for whom British golf fans had

Agony for Bernhard Langer in 1991

Agony for Craig Stadler in 1985

longed for nearly two decades, and Jack Nicklaus, the world's best golfer who had already won seven Major championships and numerous other tournaments, faced a supreme test of their spirit and skill. The adversaries each hit the green in two shots and, whereas Jacklin's approach putt was a couple of feet shy of the hole, Nicklaus rolled his ball several feet past. In terminal silence he holed the return and then picked up Jacklin's marker to signal a half and the first tie in Ryder Cup history. Nicklaus' gallant gesture encapsulated not only the spirit of the fixture but also the American's own sense of golfing chivalry.

The recent matches have been so closely fought that no one should rule out another nerve-stretching finish; a finish which might be influenced by just one unforseeable factor. One remembers Bernard Gallacher's illness at

Profile points: Ballesteros and Olazabal have forged one of the most successful partnerships in the history of the Ryder Cup

Muirfield in 1973 after the first day's play when Britain were leading by three clear points and deserving every one of them. Gallacher's absence on the second day certainly deflated the British team's confidence. In 1985 at The Belfry, Craig Stadler missed a tiny putt on the final green in his fourball match with Curtis Strange against Bernhard Langer and Sandy Lyle. The European pair won an unexpected half point and the whole psychological balance of the fixture tilted towards Europe.

Above all, the 18th hole at The Belfry, which demands both a drive and a second shot across water, is enough to shred the capabilities of even the most accomplished golfer. Andy North in 1985 and, four years later, Nick Faldo, Payne Stewart and Mark Calcavecchia all found the drink on the final hole and lost their matches. 'They're only human,' said Europe's captain, Tony Jacklin, with some feeling.

These are the unpredictable human factors, the imponderables, which can decide the fate of the Ryder Cup.

What is predictable is that many familiar names will answer the call to the Ryder Cup colours. It is impossible to imagine a European team without Severiano Ballesteros. Although he made a faltering debut in 1979, when he suffered mightily at the hands of Larry Nelson who beat him four times, and did not play two years later, Ballesteros' record since then has been remarkable. In 25 matches he has recorded 16 victories and five halves and has only suffered four defeats. He has been the most influential Ryder Cup player of the last decade, a talisman who is vital to the European cause not only for his unparalleled skills and vibrant will to win - it is no wonder that Tom Kite once said of

A view of the famous 10th green at The Belfry

Barry Lane is likely to be making his Cup debut at The Belfry in September

reinforced by four other champions: Nick Faldo, Bernhard Langer, Sandy Lyle and Ian Woosnam. The time has probably come to split up the Faldo/Woosnam partnership, once so successful but so disappointing at Kiawah Island. European supporters will also hope that Woosnam breaks his duck in the singles; five defeats out of five is hardly a reflection of his ability. The debutantes of 1991, Colin Montgomerie and Steve Richardson, will almost certainly make the team as will Barry Lane, and it may then be a matter of perming three from Ronan Rafferty, Mark James, Jamie Spence, Robert Karlsson, Anders Forsbrand, David Gilford, José Rivero and Gordon Brand Jr.

The American opposition will have plenty of power in the engine room with, one assumes, the formidable presences of Fred Couples, Davis Love, John Cook, Corey Pavin, Tom Kite, Paul Azinger, Payne Stewart and Mark O'Meara. The American selection formula has been weighted this time to take more account of current form in order to avoid a repetition of the problem caused by Wayne Levi's loss of form in 1991. His performances in the previous year won him his Ryder Cup place but by September 1991 his form and his confidence were in tatters. When he came out of the hat in the singles against Ballesteros he must have been tempted to pull a diplomatic fetlock.

No doubt there will be one or two American players whose names do not come so trippingly off the tongue; Brad Faxon, Lee Janzen, Dan Forsman or Duffy Waldorf could well make the trip to The Belfry. The team may also be reinforced by one or two veterans, perhaps even by Raymond Floyd, who was in 13th position on the US PGA money list at the end of the 1992 season. If he makes the side at the age of 51 it will be a remarkable testimony to his longevity as a

Ballesteros, 'he hits shots I never even dream about' - but also for the effect he has on the rest of the European team. This has particularly been seen in his potent partnership with fellow Spaniard, José-Maria Olazabal; in foursomes and fourballs they have won nine matches since 1987 and have only lost once.

The Spanish pair will undoubtedly be

professional golfer. He made his first appearance in 1969 and only Dai Rees will have had as long a span in the Ryder Cup (1937 to 1961). One of the 40-plus campaigners such as Lanny Wadkins, Bruce Lietzke, Craig Stadler or Ben Crenshaw might also make the team.

At Kiawah Island, the fervour of the players and their supporters, with the attendant publicity which surrounds all the great sporting occasions, at times went beyond reasonable bounds. There is surely no place for military-style forage caps at the Ryder Cup, nor for comparing a game of golf with the death and destruction of the Gulf War. The captains, Bernard Gallacher and Tom Watson, will no doubt play their parts in restraining any of the wilder excesses. The American leader will certainly bring a much-needed sense of balance, and a touch even of the Corinthian spirit to the proceedings; a stark contrast then to the combative attitude of his predecessor, Dave Stockton. Let us hope, too, that the spectators enter into the true spirit of the occasion; partisan encouragement and applause is only acceptable as long as it does not degenerate into ill-mannered abuse of the opposing players.

The Ryder Cup match at The Belfry in September will in all probability be as closely contested and dramatic as ever. It may even go to the last putt on the last green in the last match. Bernhard Langer will have everyone's sympathy if he asks his captain for a place near the top of the singles order on the final day.

And if Sam Ryder is perched on some celestial height in September, he will be astonished at the modern Ryder Cup spectacle: at the huge crush of spectators; at the intense coverage by television and the rest of the media; at the sponsorship and the

Legends and ambassadors: Nicklaus and Watson

millionaire status of the current golfing superstars. One hopes, too, that he will be uplifted by the occasion, that he will feel that his original concept of a spirited and friendly match between two teams of the best golfers in the world has been maintained or even enhanced.

Malcolm Hamer is the author of 'The Ryder Cup - The Players'.

THE 29TH RYDER CUP

27-29 September 1991 · Kiawah Island

· · · · · · · · · · · · ·

USA MATCHES		EUROPE MATCHES	
Foursomes: Morning			
P. Azinger & C. Beck	0	S. Ballesteros & J.-M. Olazabal (2 & 1)	1
R. Floyd & F. Couples (2 & 1)	1	B. Langer & M. James	0
L. Wadkins & H. Irwin (4 & 2)	1	D. Gilford & C. Montgomerie	0
P. Stewart & M. Calcavecchia (1 hole)	1	N. Faldo & I. Woosnam	0
Fourballs: Afternoon			
L. Wadkins & M. O'Meara	½	S. Torrance & D. Feherty	½
P. Azinger & C. Beck	0	S. Ballesteros & J.-M. Olazabal (2 & 1)	1
C. Pavin & M. Calcavecchia	0	S. Richardson & M. James (5 & 4)	1
R. Floyd & F. Couples (5 & 3)	1	N. Faldo & I. Woosnam	0
Foursomes: Morning			
L. Wadkins & H. Irwin (4 & 2)	1	D. Feherty & S. Torrance	0
M. Calcavecchia & P. Stewart (1 hole)	1	M. James & S. Richardson	0
P. Azinger & M. O'Meara (7 & 6)	1	N. Faldo & D. Gilford	0
R. Floyd & F. Couples	0	S. Ballesteros & J.-M. Olazabal (3 & 2)	1
Fourballs: Afternoon			
P. Azinger & H. Irwin	0	I. Woosnam & P. Broadhurst (2 & 1)	1
C. Pavin & S. Pate	0	B. Langer & C. Montgomerie (2 & 1)	1
L. Wadkins & W. Levi	0	M. James & S. Richardson (3 & 1)	1
P. Stewart & F. Couples	½	S. Ballesteros & J.-M. Olazabal	½
Singles:			
S. Pate (withdrew injured)	½	D. Gilford	½
R. Floyd	0	N. Faldo (2 holes)	1
P. Stewart	0	D. Feherty (2 & 1)	1
M. Calcavecchia	½	C. Montgomerie	½
P. Azinger (2 holes)	1	J.-M. Olazabal	0
C. Pavin (2 & 1)	1	S. Richardson	0
W. Levi	0	S. Ballesteros (3 & 2)	1
C. Beck (3 & 1)	1	I. Woosnam	0
M. O'Meara	0	P. Broadhurst (3 & 1)	1
F. Couples (3 & 2)	1	S. Torrance	0
L. Wadkins (3 & 2)	1	M. James	0
H. Irwin	½	B. Langer	½
USA 14 ½		**EUROPE 13½**	

Samuel Ryder's great gift to golf

RYDER CUP HISTORY

UNITED STATES 22, GREAT BRITAIN/EUROPE 5, TIES 2

1927	Worcester CC, Worcester, Mass.	US 9½, Britain 2½
1929	Moortown, Yorkshire, England	Britain 7, US 5
1931	Scioto CC, Columbus, Ohio	US 9, Britain 3
1933	Southport & Ainsdale, England	Britain 6 ½, US 5½
1935	Ridgewood CC, Ridgewood, NJ	US 9, Britain 3
1937	Southport & Ainsdale, England	US 8, Britain 4
	Ryder Cup not contested during World War II	
1947	Portland Golf Club, Portland, Ore	US 11, Britain 1
1949	Ganton GC, Scarborough, England	US 7, Britain 5
1951	Pinehurst CC, Pinehurst, NC	US 9½, Britain 2½
1953	Wentworth, Surrey, England	US 6½, Britain 5½
1955	Thunderbird Ranch & CC, Palm Springs, Ca.	
		US 8, Britain 4
1957	Lindrick GC, Yorkshire, England	Britain 7½, US 4½
1959	Eldorado CC, Palm Desert, Ca.	US 8½, Britain 3½
1961	Royal Lytham & St Anne's GC, St Anne's-on-the-Sea, England	US 14½, Britain 9½
1963	East Lake CC, Atlanta, Ga.	US 23, Britain 9
1965	Royal Birkdale GC, Southport, England	
		US 19½, Britain 12½
1967	Champions GC, Houston, Tex.	US 23½, Britain 8½
1969	Royal Birkdale GC, Southport, England	
		US 16, Britain 16 (TIE)
1971	Old Warson CC, St Louis, Mo.	US 18½, Britain 13½
1973	Muirfield, Scotland	US 18, Britain 13
1975	Laurel Valley GC, Ligonier, Pa.	US 21, Britain 11
1977	Royal Lytham & St Anne's GC, St Anne's-on-the-Sea, England	US 12½, Britain 7½
1979	The Greenbrier, White Sulphur Springs, W. Va.	
		US 17, Europe 11
1981	Walton Heath GC, Surrey, England	US 18½, Europe 9½
1983	PGA National GC, Palm Beach Gdns, Fla.	
		US 14½ Europe 13½
1985	The Belfry, Sutton Coldfield, England	
		Europe 16½, US 11½
1987	Muirfield Village, Ohio	Europe 15, US 13
1989	The Belfry, Sutton Coldfield, England	
		Europe 14, US 14 (TIE)
1991	Kiawah Island, South Carolina	US 14½, Europe 13½

Two celebrated European links: (above) sunrise at Noordwijkse in Holland,
and overleaf, sunset over the Old Course at Ballybunion
in South West Ireland

6

GREAT GOLF COURSES
OF THE WORLD

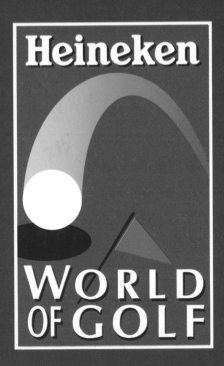

GREAT GOLF COURSES
OF THE WORLD

Pity the sportsmen and women who play their game on a pitch or a court
and whose surroundings never vary. And pity the golfer who must
concentrate in surroundings such as these! (Above) the incredible
lunar-like setting at La Quinta, California; (below) Augusta, golf's own
Garden of Eden and (opposite) 'Sussex by the Sea': clear sky at Rye,
and can't you almost smell the salty air?

Golf beneath the shadows of Mount Fuji, Japan and (inset) where kangaroos caddy – the Kooralbyn Country Club, Queensland, Australia

(Above) Chateau golf: the Royal and Ancient game has taken France by storm. French clubhouses are often grand affairs and the Chateau de Vigiers at Monestier near Bordeaux is a good example. It is also a place where that phrase 'Fancy a drink at the 19th?' takes on a new dimension. (Left) Reflections 'Down Under': The Australian Golf Club near Sydney, and (right) 'Out of Africa': the Gary Player Country Club at Bophuthatswana, where millions of dollars are regularly won, lost and sometimes thrown away